Fitzgerald v. Nita & Western Railroad

Fifth Edition

FITZGERALD V. NITA & WESTERN RAILROAD

Fifth Edition

Laurence M. Rose

NITA®
NATIONAL INSTITUTE FOR TRIAL ADVOCACY

Address inquiries to:
Reprint Permission
National Institute for Trial Advocacy
1685 38th Street, Suite 200
Boulder, CO 80301-2735
Phone: (800) 225-6482
Fax: (720) 890-7069
E-mail: permissions@nita.org

ISBN 978-1-60156-480-1 (print)
eISBN 978-1-60156-515-0 (eBook)
FBA 1480

Printed in the United States of America

Contents

Acknowledgments

My advocacy teaching over the years has been supported by many judges, lawyers, professors, and laypeople. In particular, I would like to recognize Bob Stein, JoAnne Epps, Dominic Gianna, and Frank Rothschild for their friendship, support, and assistance. I especially dedicate this edition to the late Jo Ann Harris and the late Jim R. Carrigan.

I wish to acknowledge my University of Miami School of Law deans, Mary Doyle, Sam Thompson, Dennis Lynch, and Trish White, for their continued support of me, my program, and my desire to have an impact on the teaching of trial advocacy to law students and attorneys.

The expert witness reports and analyses were contributed by William F. Landsea, PhD, Professor Emeritus of the University of Miami, who also provided indispensable advice on the economic issues presented in this case. I extend my appreciation to University of Kansas Professor Gary Mason for his valuable assistance in the production of the photographs used in this case file.

I continue to express my gratitude to the University of Kansas School of Law for support of my work on the first edition during my sabbatical leave.

Finally, and of most importance, my appreciation and gratitude to my wonderful family: Amy, my ever-supportive wife; my children and their spouses: Josh and Randi, Mark, Mike and Amanda, Emily and Natalie; and especially to my four exceptional grandchildren: Corey, Alex, Jacob, and Cami.

Laurence M. Rose

Miami, Florida

2015

Introduction

Fitzgerald v. Nita & Western Railroad is a wrongful death action arising out of an accident at a railroad crossing. The accident occurred on October 20, 2013, at about 5:47 p.m. at Crossing No. 74647C, located at the intersection of County Road and the main line tracks of the Nita & Western Railroad. The weather was clear and visibility was good.

The plaintiffs are the Estate of Johnny Fitzgerald and his surviving family. They contend that the railroad was negligent in not providing adequate warnings and proper maintenance at the crossing and in the operation of the train.

The defendant contends that Johnny Fitzgerald was negligent in the operation of his car or that he intentionally drove his car into the train.

Discovery has been completed, and each side has disclosed to the other all information that is in this case file, including memoranda to counsel and photographs.

This case file is designed to be used as a comparative negligence trial file, a negotiation file, or a fact investigation file.

Instructions for Use

Issues for Trial

This case file may be used for a trial on the issue of liability only or for both issues of liability and damages. If used solely for the issue of liability, the proposed jury instructions should be modified accordingly by deleting instructions 22 and 23, modifying the verdict form, and deleting the testimony of the plaintiffs' and defendant's experts (William Landsea and Robert O'Sullivan).

Witnesses

When this case file is used for a full trial, the following witnesses are available to the parties:

Plaintiff	Defendant
Debra Fitzgerald	Mark Edwards
Stacy Beck	Steve Smolen
Michael Benjamin	Emily Field
David Jonathan	Joshua Alan
William Landsea	Robert O'Sullivan

A party need not call all of the witnesses listed as its witnesses. Any or all of the witnesses may be called by either party, subject to the limitation that neither party may call more than five witnesses. If a witness is to be called by a party other than the one for whom he/she is listed, the party for whom the witness is listed will select and prepare the witness.

The following witnesses may appear by deposition or statement only and can be introduced by either party:

Ethel Kay

Matt Green

Paul Field

Amy Field

Nick Baron

The exhibits throughout the case file and those highlighted in the PowerPoint slide show are designated:

PX (Plaintiffs' Exhibit)

DX (Defendant's Exhibit)

JX (Joint Exhibit)

Required Stipulations

1. The statements made in the edited depositions are admissible to the same extent as statements from full depositions.
2. Nita City is a fairly large city. Approximately thirty miles to the southeast is the rural town of Wellington (pop. 15,000). Marion is at the far southwest corner of the state of Nita, approximately 250 miles from Wellington.
3. Rich April (N&W conductor) no longer works for Nita & Western Railroad and cannot be located.
4. The letters from the State of Nita and Douglas County (PX-6, PX-7) are authentic and are admissible under FRE 803(8), which has been adopted in Nita.
5. October 20, 2013, was a Sunday.
6. Multiplying 1.47 times the miles per hour a vehicle is traveling will give you the feet per second that vehicle is traveling.
7. Annotations have been added to the scene photographs in the PowerPoint slideshow to more clearly indicate when the photos were taken and/or from what vantage point they were taken relative to the crossing. In addition, Joint Exhibit 21 (JX 21) has been created to clarify at what distance from the crossing various photographic exhibits were taken.

IN THE CIRCUIT COURT OF
DOUGLAS COUNTY, NITA
CIVIL DIVISION

DEBRA FITZGERALD, Administratrix of the Estate of JOHNNY FITZGERALD, and DEBRA FITZGERALD, individually and on behalf of her minor child NATALIE FITZGERALD Plaintiffs v. NITA & WESTERN RAILROAD CO. Defendant	))))))))))))))	COMPLAINT

Plaintiffs for their complaint against Defendant allege:

1. At all times material, the plaintiffs are and were residents of Wellington, Douglas County, Nita.
2. Plaintiff Debra Fitzgerald was appointed administratrix of the Estate of Johnny Fitzgerald by the Probate Court of Douglas County, Nita, on November 15, 2013, and is the widow of Johnny Fitzgerald; Natalie Fitzgerald is the daughter of Johnny Fitzgerald and Debra Fitzgerald.
3. Defendant Nita & Western Railroad Co. is a corporation organized and existing under the laws of the State of Nita, with a principal place of business in Nita City, Nita.
4. On October 20, 2013, at approximately 5:47 p.m., Johnny Fitzgerald was operating an automobile on County Road in Douglas County, Nita, in an easterly direction, approaching railroad crossing #74647C.
5. At this time and place, the defendant, acting through its agents and employees, was operating a freight train in a northerly direction on railroad tracks belonging to the defendant.
6. At the intersection of said road and tracks, the vehicle operated by Johnny Fitzgerald was in a collision with the train operated by the defendant, and as a result of the collision, Johnny Fitzgerald suffered severe injuries, which caused his death.
7. The collision and resulting death of Johnny Fitzgerald was solely caused by the negligence of the defendant in failing to adequately and timely warn Johnny Fitzgerald of the oncoming train, in failing to properly maintain the intersecting roadway foliage, in operating the train at an unsafe speed, and in failing to maintain a proper lookout.

8. Prior to his death, Johnny Fitzgerald was a healthy individual, capable of and supporting his wife and minor child. As a result of his death, Debra Fitzgerald and Natalie Fitzgerald have been deprived of:
   a. The reasonably expected net income of Johnny Fitzgerald;
   b. Services, protection, care, and assistance of Johnny Fitzgerald, whether voluntary or obligatory;
   c. Society, companionship, comfort, guidance, kindly offices, and advice of Johnny Fitzgerald.
9. As a result of his death, the Estate of Johnny Fitzgerald has incurred reasonable funeral and burial expenses in the amount of $5,000.

Wherefore, the plaintiffs demand judgment against the defendant, Nita & Western Railroad Co., in the amount of $8,000,000 together with interest thereon, costs of this action, and for such other relief as the Court deems just and proper.

Plaintiffs demand trial by jury in this action.

Debra Fitzgerald,

By

Thomas Bush

Thomas Busch
Attorney for Plaintiffs
2000 Johnson Drive
Wellington, Nita

Dated: December 12, 2013

Return of Summons

I hereby certify that the above complaint was personally served on James Bell, president and authorized process agent for Nita & Western Railroad Co.

James Brown
Process Server

Dated: December 15, 2013

IN THE CIRCUIT COURT OF
DOUGLAS COUNTY, NITA
CIVIL DIVISION

DEBRA FITZGERALD, Administratrix of the Estate of JOHNNY FITZGERALD, and DEBRA FITZGERALD, individually and on behalf of her minor child NATALIE FITZGERALD Plaintiffs v. NITA & WESTERN RAILROAD CO. Defendant	))))))))))))))	ANSWER

The defendant for its answer to the plaintiffs' complaint:

1. Admits the allegations contained in paragraphs 1–6.
2. Denies the allegations of paragraph 7.
3. Is without sufficient knowledge or information to form a belief as to the truth of the allegations of paragraphs 8 and 9, and therefore denies them.

Affirmative Defenses

4. Any injuries sustained or suffered by Johnny Fitzgerald at the time and place mentioned in the plaintiffs' complaint (and therefore any resulting injuries suffered by the plaintiffs) were caused in whole or in part, or were contributed to, by the negligence and/or intentional act of Johnny Fitzgerald and not by any negligence on the part of the defendant.

Wherefore, the defendant requests that judgment be entered in its favor in this action, together with costs of this action and for such other relief as the Court deems just and proper.

Defendant demands trial by jury.

By

John Colton

John Colton Colton & McLeod
Regency Plaza, Suite 1300 Nita City, Nita

Dated: December 22, 2013

Certificate of Service

I hereby certify that on December 22, 2013, a copy of the above Answer was placed in the United States mail, postage prepaid, addressed to Thomas Busch, Attorney for the Plaintiff, 2000 Johnson Drive, Wellington, Nita.

John Colton

Colton & McLeod

Deposition of Debra Fitzgerald*

March 16, 2014

My name is Debra Fitzgerald, but everyone calls me Debi. I was born on November 19, 1990, in Nita City. I live at 16 Meadowbrook Lane in Wellington, Nita, with my daughter, Natalie, who was born on May 22, 2008. I am the widow of Johnny Fitzgerald, who died on October 20, 2013, six days short of his twenty-fifth birthday.

I grew up in Nita City and lived with my parents, Ethel and Irv Kay, throughout high school. I attended Nita City High, but did not finish. Johnny and I were married at my parents' home in Nita City on January 3, 2008. I received my GED online after I got married and went to City Tech for some business courses after Natalie was eighteen months old. I hope to become an administrative assistant as soon as I finish school. I expect to go back to City Tech as soon as I get enough money.

At the time of my husband's death, I was working the 4:00 to 8:00 p.m. shift at the Flinders Aluminum plant, helping in the stockroom with inventory. It was a temporary job during the fall. I always tried to have some extra money for special things. I usually worked the late afternoons so that Johnny could watch Natalie when he came home from work. He worked the 7:00 a.m. to 3:00 p.m. shift at the new Uprite Scaffolding plant as a welder. At the time of his death, he was earning approximately $800 per week. Johnny's income went to pay all of the bills for the house, the food, and all the necessary things. My paycheck was for extra things and for presents, such as the new shotgun I had bought as a surprise present for Johnny's birthday, but didn't get a chance to give to him. We didn't have a lot of money in the bank, but we were comfortable.

We were a very happy family. Johnny and I were best friends and always had a great time together. We cared for each other a great deal and hardly ever fought. Johnny was devoted to Natalie. He would always read to her at night and take long walks with her before dinner. He was especially good to her and was always taking her with him on trips to the supermarket, the library, and department stores for presents for birthdays and holidays. As a matter of fact, Johnny had taken Natalie

* The transcript of Debra Fitzgerald's deposition was excerpted so that only her answers are reprinted here. Assume that this is a true and accurate rendering of those answers.

to buy a new costume for Halloween, and my dad had to take her out on Halloween because I just couldn't do it. Natalie really missed her dad that night. She still does.

We spent a lot of time with my parents. Johnny and my dad did a lot of work renovating the den at my parents' home. He loved to work with his hands and help people. He was just that type of person. At the time of his death, Johnny was in good health, and so were the rest of us.

He was enjoying his job and had just received his five-year pin for being with Uprite. He was looking forward to his ten-year pin and had recently talked about the retirement benefits to which he had just become entitled.

Johnny also enjoyed his high school friends from Wellington High, especially his best friend, Paul Field. Johnny was the best man at Paul's wedding on July 4, 2012. We spent a lot of time with Johnny's friends whenever they came home. We even went camping with some of them sometimes. I really didn't care for camping much, but because Johnny liked it, we went together. Since Johnny's friends were mostly guys, I became friends with their girlfriends or wives. I knew that Johnny was friendly with all of them before we started dating, but I was never considered an outsider. Johnny and Emily Field (Paul's wife) had dated each other before we were married, but had broken up just before Johnny and I started dating. They continued to be very friendly, and sometimes I was concerned about their relationship. During a camping trip in August 2011 with Paul and Emily, about a year before they got married, I saw Johnny and Emily talking very quietly while Paul and I were cooking dinner.

Later that evening, Johnny had told me that Emily had asked him to take her for a walk where they could (as he told me that Emily said) "see the stars one more time together." I was shocked and told Johnny that I wanted to go home immediately, but Johnny said not to worry, that she was just fooling around and probably wasn't serious. Even if she was, Johnny said he was in love with me and Natalie, and he didn't want anything to affect our wonderful family. After that night, I just couldn't get real close to Emily. I was always thinking that she felt I took Johnny away from her and that she married Paul just to stay close to Johnny.

On Saturday, October 19, the day before Johnny died, we went to visit Paul and Emily, who had come to stay with Paul's mother and father, Amy and Lonny. The Fields had come to Wellington to help celebrate the birthday of Greg Carlisle, a friend of Paul and Johnny from high school. Since Emily and Paul lived in Marion, we only got to see them a few times a year. They brought their new baby girl, Cameron, who we hadn't seen yet. We had gotten to Mrs. Field's house about 5:30 p.m. We expected to stay over and sleep in the downstairs guest room. The guys, Johnny, Paul, and Greg, played pool downstairs while Emily, the baby, Natalie, and I stayed upstairs with Paul's mother. The children played while we watched television. At about 8:00 p.m. the guys went out to have dinner and some beer while we got the children ready for bed. Emily needed some diapers for the baby, so I went with her in her car to the store. We got back in about twenty minutes, at about 9:10 p.m. Emily fed the baby, and we put the children to sleep. About 9:30 p.m. Emily and I went to meet the guys at Rocco's. We had one or two beers while we were there, danced to the music, and had a pretty good time. Johnny danced with Emily and I danced with Paul for one dance, and then Johnny and Emily talked a little in the corner booth. When Johnny came back, I asked him what they talked about, and he said that Emily wanted to know what she should buy Johnny for his birthday. We stayed until about 10:45 when Emily had to go home to nurse the baby. While she was feeding the baby, I checked on Natalie, who was asleep, and then I watched TV alone. At about midnight, Johnny and Paul came home. Paul was feeling the effects of the beer, and Johnny had to help him into the house. After getting Paul into his room, Johnny said he wanted to go home and sleep in our bed rather than stay over, so I collected Natalie and our things and Johnny drove us home. Johnny appeared to be in good spirits and said that he expected that Paul would sleep late, so there was no reason to stay overnight. Johnny did not have a lot to drink and drove home carefully. As a matter of fact, Johnny did not like to drink.

On the day he died, Natalie and I woke up late, after Johnny was already up. I was still tired from getting home late from visiting the Fields.

Q. What happened after breakfast?

A. Johnny and Natalie went out for a walk, and I cleaned the dishes. At about
ten o'clock, I called Emily and Paul to thank them for the night before.

Q. Tell me exactly what you told them during that phone call.

A. I only talked with Emily. Paul was still sleeping.

Q. What did you say to Emily?

A. Like I said, I thanked the two of them for such a nice visit the night before. Then I asked Emily to have Paul call Johnny after he got up to say goodbye before they left town.

Q. Did you say anything else to Emily during that phone conversation?

A. No, it was just a quick call.

Q. What happened after Johnny and Natalie came back from their walk?

A. I told Johnny that since he wanted to watch football games on TV all day, I was going to take Natalie to Nita City to visit my parents, do some laundry, and maybe catch a movie.

Q. When did you leave to go to your parents?

A. I remember Johnny went to get a newspaper at noon, so it must have been about 12:30 when we left.

Q. What did you take with you?

A. Just the laundry.

Q. Which was in what?

A. An overnight case.

Q. You mean a piece of luggage?

A. Yes, a small suitcase.

We got there about 1:15 p.m. and talked for a while. Then I took Natalie to a movie. We got back about 4:30 and helped with dinner. About 5:30 p.m. I received a text from Johnny. It said, "Hope you and Natalie are having a good day. I Love You, J." It was a little odd because he never called himself "J." Here is a copy of the text message he sent me (PX 11).

After dinner, my dad took Natalie for a walk. Around 7 p.m., I got a call from Emily on my cell phone. She had tried us at the house, but there was no answer. She wanted to say goodbye to Johnny. I said that he wasn't with me at my parents' house, that he had stayed at home, but maybe he went out for a pizza. I told Emily that we would see her the next time they visited, and she said goodbye. Then I left Natalie with my parents and went downstairs to do the laundry. The first I knew about the accident was about 7:30 p.m. My mom came downstairs and told me that Johnny had been killed by a train. I fainted and was in the hospital for a few days because I was in shock.

The funeral was shortly after that, but I really don't remember much about it. I was in a fog the whole time. Natalie and I got some help in handling the house after Johnny died, and his company's life insurance money has kept us going. It will run out soon, and I hope to get a job as soon as I can finish my administrative assistant training. Here is a copy of the funeral bill (PX 1).

Right now I have to take care of Natalie. She misses her daddy very much. Some friends have been very helpful, especially Linda Roth and Chuck Reynolds. Chuck was my supervisor at the Flinders Aluminum plant, and we have become very close friends. He has been extremely good to Natalie.

The accident occurred about eight or nine miles from where we live. I don't think that Johnny had ever been on that road before, but I can't be sure. The road leads to the new Uprite plant, but Johnny usually took the main road to get to work. I know this because I sometimes drove Johnny to work, and he said that the main road was faster and shorter from our house. He had hunted in the general area of the plant before it was built, and maybe he had gone out there to find a place for hunting. Pheasant season began on October 28, and I know that Paul and Johnny had made plans to go hunting.

Johnny's car was a 2002 Ford, but it was in good shape. Johnny did all the work on it himself to save money. About two weeks before the accident, he had a problem with his brakes and did a whole brake job on the car. In fact, Johnny also tuned up the engine and adjusted all of the hoses and things in preparation for the winter. I don't think that anything went wrong with the car. Johnny was a careful driver, too. He never went too fast, although he did not always stay within the speed limit. No one really does. The only reason for this accident that makes any sense is that the railroad did something wrong.

No, Johnny and I had never talked about a separation, divorce, or anything like that. We were a very happy couple. You can see that in this photo I brought. It was taken New Year's Eve 2012 (PX 12).

I have read this deposition, and the answers are correct to the best of my knowledge and belief.

Debra Fitzgerald

Debra Fitzgerald

Harold Bench

Harold Bench

Notary Public

March 16, 2014

PX 1

Erickson Mortuary

Since 1902

12 Main Street
Wellington, Nita
(515) 264-0003

Statement

Debra Fitzgerald

16 Meadowbrook Lane

Wellington, Nita

For services rendered:

Transportation, October 20, 2013

Preparation and Chapel, October 20–23, 2013

Transportation and Burial, October 23, 2013 $5,000.00

Payment received November 27, 2013

By

Melissa Ryan

Erickson Mortuary

A family-owned enterprise for three generations, the Erickson Mortuary staff and family of founder Edward L. Erickson wish you the comfort of memories and peace that comes with time. Thank you for allowing us this opportunity to be of service to you and your loved ones.

Deposition of Ethel Kay*

April 15, 2014

My name is Ethel Kay, and I am fifty-five years old. I live at 211 Bluebell in Nita City with my husband, Irv. My daughter is Debra Fitzgerald. She is my only child.

Debra is a fine girl, and she is a very good mother to Natalie, my granddaughter. Debi was a good student in high school and received good grades. She was never a problem to us when she was growing up. In high school, she got to be very friendly with a group of people in Wellington, where we had a summer house. I really didn't care for the people there, but they were nice to us. She dated a little while we were down there, but nothing serious until the fall of 2007, when she began to date Johnny Fitzgerald. He was a nice boy, although not like the boys Debi dated from Nita City. We didn't disapprove of him, but we didn't really encourage her either. In late December, Debi and Johnny came to us and told us that Debi was pregnant. Needless to say, we were upset, but felt we had to support our little girl. We quickly arranged a wedding, and they were married in our home on January 3, 2008. Natalie was born May 22.

Debi and Johnny were happy, and they both loved their daughter. I never knew them to fight or argue, and they have always loved to spend time with each other. Johnny was a good provider and worked hard. He loved to work with his hands and always helped us around the house, even helping my husband finish our den. Johnny and Debi spent a lot of time with us, and they had a bedroom in our house so that they could stay over anytime. Both of them came to see us whenever they were in Nita City together, and sometimes one or the other would come up to spend time. While Johnny was working or hunting, Debi might visit, and when Debi was working, Johnny might bring Natalie for dinner. It was a very happy situation.

On Sunday morning, October 20, 2013, Debi called to say that she and Natalie were coming up to visit that day. Debi wanted to take Natalie to a movie in the afternoon and then have dinner with us. Johnny was going to watch the football game on TV. She arrived at our house about 1:15 p.m. Debi

* The transcript of Ethel Kay's deposition was excerpted so that only her answers are reprinted here. Assume that this is a true and accurate rendering of those answers.

and Natalie visited for a while and then went to the movie. They came back about 4:30 and helped me prepare dinner. We had our dinner, and Natalie and my husband went out for a walk about 6:00 p.m. and came back right after sunset. Debi looked like she wanted to talk about something, but she did not say anything. At about 7:00 Debi's cell phone rang. She talked for about two minutes. I asked who it was, and she said it was their friends, the Fields, who were looking for Johnny to say goodbye. Debi and Johnny had spent the day with the Fields on Saturday, and Paul and Emily were going back to Marion early the next morning. Debi wondered where Johnny might be, since they said they had tried to call him at home, but Debi felt he might have gone out to get something to eat.

At about 7:15, Debi went downstairs to start some laundry. About five minutes later, we got a phone call from Chief Neely of the Wellington Police Department. He said that he had heard some bad news over the radio and felt that we needed to know. He said that Johnny had been killed at a railroad crossing. I was in shock. I told my husband, and he told me to go downstairs to get Debi while he stayed with Natalie. I went downstairs and told Debi the bad news. She fainted, and I had to call an ambulance to take her to the hospital. When she woke up at the hospital, Debi asked me to call Paul and Emily at Paul's mother's house to tell them the bad news. She stayed at the hospital until Tuesday, and we watched Natalie and made the funeral arrangements. The funeral was Wednesday, but Debi was in a fog for about a week.

We have been very supportive of Debi and Natalie. She has tried to make it by herself financially, but I know it is going to be hard without some help. She has some good friends who help her emotionally. She has asked us not to give her money, only moral support. We try the best we can. For example, my husband helped by taking Natalie out on Halloween, just like her daddy was going to do.

About a week after the funeral, I wrote a letter to the editor of the Wellington newspaper about the accident and the negligence of the railroad. Yes, that is the letter (PX 2). I am amazed by the lack of care of the railroad in not putting automatic flashing lights at all of their crossings. My lawyer told me that this was gross negligence, and I asked him to recommend a lawyer in Wellington. I gave the name to Debi, and she contacted him. He is the one who filed this lawsuit.

Around the first of April, I received a phone call from Amy Field, Paul's mother. She said that her daughter-in-law, Emily, had been asked and gave a deposition in the case and she was concerned about what was going on in the case. She said that Emily didn't want to hurt Debi or Natalie, and I told her that if Emily wanted to help, she should just stay out of it. Emily was always sticking her nose into Debi and Johnny's business. I really think that she was jealous of the happiness that Johnny and Debi had together.

No, Debi never talked of leaving Johnny. Why would she say anything about that? They were very happy together. Who is saying that they were separating? No, Debi did not bring any clothes with her that night other than her laundry, and they were not planning to stay over that night. Where are you getting this from?

I have read this deposition, and the answers are correct to the best of my knowledge and belief.

Ethel Kay

Harold Bench
Notary Public

April 15, 2014

PX 2

Nita Daily Journal-News

Letter to the Editor

November 2, 2013

Editor
Nita Daily Journal-News
422 S. Rose Avenue
Nita City, Nita 49099

Dear Editor:

Something has to be done about the reckless actions of the Nita & Western Railroad in maintaining the railroad crossings in Wellington. They continually disregard the rights of innocent people when they do not upgrade. Something has to be done about crossings and install automatic safety signals at crossings that have increased traffic and lead to populated areas. Just two weeks ago my daughter lost her husband when he was run over and killed by a freight train that went through an uncontrolled crossing without taking proper precautions. Crossings like the one on County Road must be protected by flashing lights and bells to protect everyone. If the railroad doesn't begin to think of someone else besides themselves, then other people will die.

Mrs. Ethel Kay

Nita City

Transcript of Recorded Statement: Stacy Beck

November 23, 2013

This conversation is being recorded on November 23, 2013, about 3:05 p.m. It is being recorded at Route 8, Wellington, Nita. My name is Tom Busch, and I am the attorney for the Estate of Johnny Fitzgerald.

Q. Would you mind stating your full name for me, please, and spelling your last name.

A. Stacy Beck. That's B-E-C-K.

Q. Okay, I've informed you that I am a lawyer for Debra Fitzgerald and that I represent the Estate of Johnny Fitzgerald, is that correct?

A. Yes, sir.

Q. Are you aware of the fact that I am recording this conversation?

A. Yes, sir.

Q. And I have your permission?

A. Yes, sir.

Q. Okay, I'll be asking you some questions today. If I ask you anything that you don't understand, please tell me and I'll try to make it clearer. Is that okay?

A. Right.

Q. Okay. And after we have recorded the conversation, I'll play it back, and if you need to correct anything, you can do so at the end. Okay?

A. Right.

Q. What is your age?

A. Forty-one.

Q. What is your home address?

A. Route 8, Box 112C, Wellington, Nita.

Q. Okay, and that is where we are now?

A. Right.

Q. What is your occupation?

A. I am a painter, an artist.

Q. Do you work for anyone?

A. No, I'm self-employed.

Q. Where do you live with respect to the Nita & Western Railroad crossing at County Road?

A. I live northeast of the crossing, about 100 yards east of the tracks and north of County Road approximately 100 feet.

Q. I want to know if you remember the crossing accident that occurred on October 20, 2013.

A. Yes, I do.

Q. Were you at home at the time?

A. Yes.

Q. Were you a witness to the accident?

A. No.

Q. Specifically, where were you?

A. I was sitting in my living room watching the football game on the TV. It was a great game. I had the game turned up loud, and I'd had a few beers.

Q. Please describe where the living room is in relation to the railroad crossing.

A. My house runs east and west. The living room is at the east end of the house at the front, facing County Road.

Q. When did you first become aware that an accident had taken place?

A. Right before six o'clock in the evening, a car drove up to my house and a man came to my door and knocked. I answered the door, and he said, would I please call the police and an ambulance, the train had hit a car on the crossing. I had never seen him before. Then he got back into his car and drove away toward the east on County Road. I called 911 on my cell phone, gave the operator my name and address, and asked her to tell the police and ambulance to come to the crossing.

Q. Then what happened?

A. I ran outside and unhooked my dog from around the tree, cut through the field to the road, and went to the crossing. I saw the train sitting on the tracks, halfway through the crossing. North of the main body of the train was what was left of a car on the tracks, and north of that were four engines and a boxcar. I saw a man from the train walking along the tracks, and he told me that he had found a man lying near the tracks a little ways ahead and that he was dead.

Q. So based on what you just said, you didn't see either the train or the car prior to the collision?

A. No, I didn't see nothing or hear nothing.

Q. Were you aware that a train was in the area?

A. Yes, the train was going by because the house was shaking.

Q. Could you state whether or not an engine whistle was sounded?

A. There was no whistle. I didn't hear any. That was a little strange because I usually hear the 5:40 train whistle. That's the time when I usually feed the dog. And I commented to myself when the house shook, "Where's the whistle?"

Q. Could you say one way or another as to whether or not it was sounding?

A. I never heard the whistle, either before or during or after the crossing.

Q. How was the weather that afternoon?

A. It was a pretty fall day. Cool and crisp, clear and dry.

Q. What time did the sun set that day?

A. About 6:15 or so.

Q. From where you were sitting watching TV, could you have seen the crossing?

A. Not from where I was sitting.

Q. And that is because there was a wall there?

A. If I was in the bedroom I could have seen the crossing, but I wasn't in the bedroom.

Q. Did you stay at the scene?

A. I waited until the trooper arrived and the ambulance took away the man. I gave my name to the trooper and went home.

Q. What can you tell me about the traffic on County Road across the railroad crossing?

A. Well, ever since they built that new scaffolding plant in September 2012, northeast of the crossing, there have been a lot of cars going to the plant. Sometimes a truck comes looking for the plant and goes down County Road, even though it is a gravel road. Most of the traffic comes by in the morning about 6:30, and then the rest of the traffic is about 3:30 in the afternoon. I have heard of some near accidents at the crossing. I think that the crossing is unsafe without lights and bells. Why, just a few days after the accident, they came out to fix the sign and put in another crossbuck. I just knew that someone was going to get killed there someday.

Q. Would you please draw on this piece of paper a diagram showing your house and the railroad crossing?

A. Sure (PX 3).

Q. Tell you what, let me stop this and play it back, we'll listen to it, and if there is anything you need to correct, we can take care of it at the end. All right?

A. All right.

Q. Okay, we have played the recording back and listened to it, have we not?

A. Yes.

Q. Is it correct to the best of your knowledge?

A. That's right.

Q. Is there anything further you want to add?

A. Nothing.

Q. Okay, thank you very much.

Transcribed at Wellington, Nita

November 29, 2013

PX 3

Map of Stacy Beck's Residence and Adjacent Railroad

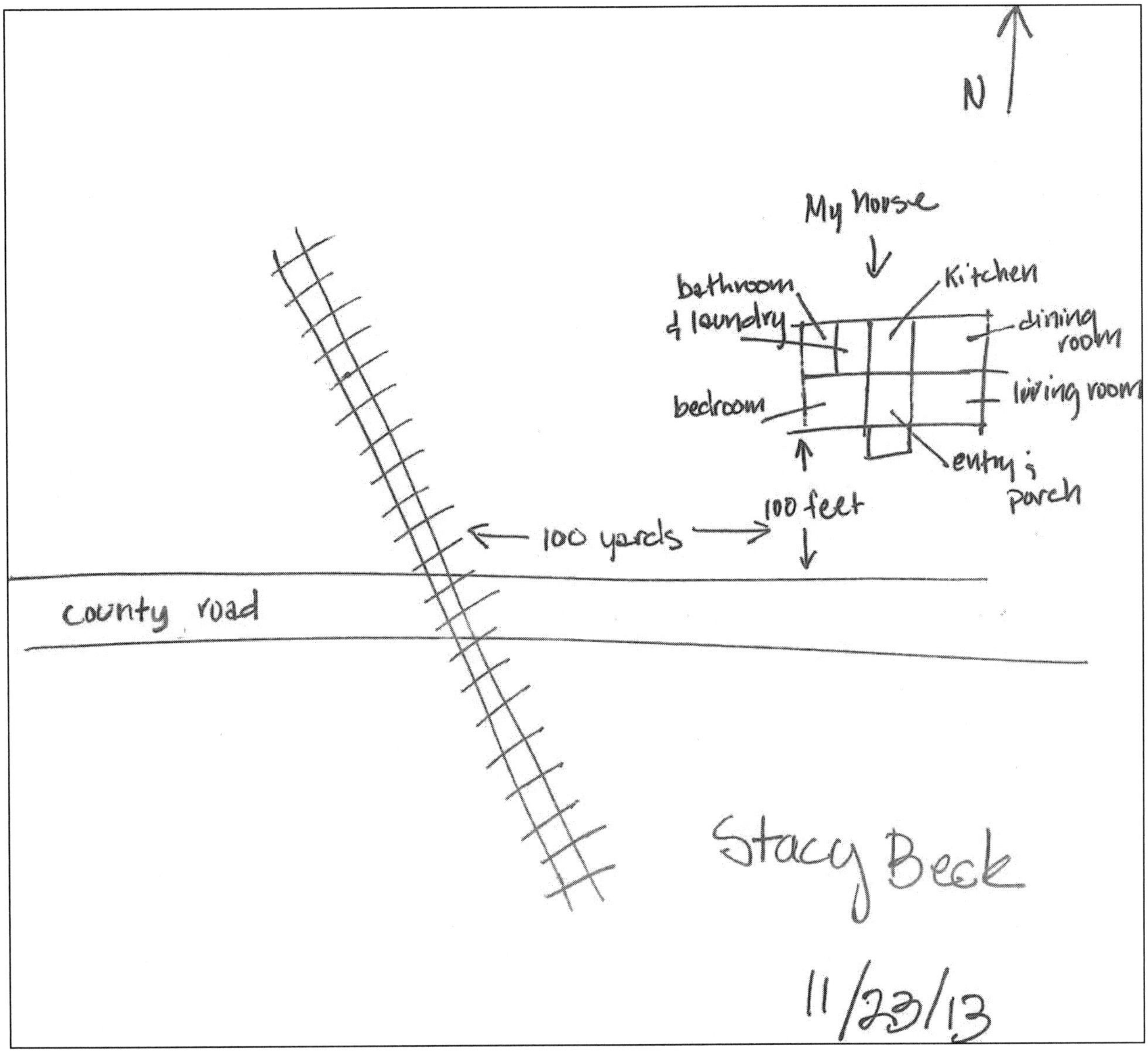

JX 18

Vehicle Accident Report

INVESTIGATOR'S MOTOR VEHICLE ACCIDENT REPORT

TOTAL NUMBER OF VEHICLES INVOLVED: 2

DATE OF ACCIDENT	MONTH: 10	DAY: 20	YEAR: 13
DAY OF ACCIDENT	SUN: X		
TIME OF ACCIDENT	MILITARY TIME: 1747 HRS.		
FOR STATE USE ONLY			
PLACE WHERE ACCIDENT OCCURRED	COUNTY: DOUGLAS	CITY, TOWN OR TOWNSHIP: WELLINGTON	ACCIDENT OCCURRED ON PRIVATE PROPERTY: ☐
ROAD ON WHICH ACCIDENT OCCURRED	GIVE NAME OF STREET OR HIGHWAY NO.: (U.S. or State)(If no highway number, identify by name): COUNTY ROAD	POSTED SPEED LIMIT: 50	
DISTANCE FROM MILEPOST	FEET: N S E W	OF MILEPOST: No.	HIGHWAY NUMBER: Dist.

IF AT INTERSECTION	IF NOT AT INTERSECTION		
NAME OF INTERSECTING STREET OR HIGHWAY NO.:	FEET: AT	N S E W	SHOW NEAREST INTERSECTING STREET OR HIGHWAY, HOUSE NUMBER, BRIDGE, RAILROAD CROSSING, UNDERPASS, OR MILEPOST: Railroad Crossing #74647C
IF ACCIDENT WAS OUTSIDE CITY LIMITS, INDICATE DISTANCE FROM NEAREST TOWN	MILES: 1.5	N S E W: X (W)	AND MILES: N S E W OF NEAREST CITY OR TOWN: Wellington

VEHICLE—1	VEHICLE—2
DRIVER: (Print or Type Full Name) Johnny Fitzgerald	DRIVER: (Print or Type Full Name) Steve Smolen
PHONE:	PHONE:
DRIVER'S ADDRESS: (Street or R.F.D.) 16 Meadowbrook	DRIVER'S ADDRESS: (Street or R.F.D.) 449 Clearmeadow
CITY, STATE AND ZIP CODE: Wellington, NT	CITY, STATE AND ZIP CODE: Nita City, NT
DRIVER'S LICENSE: DATE OF BIRTH MO. 10 DAY 26 YR. 88; NUMBER: NT W3F1R4; STATE: NT; ■ MALE ☐ FEMALE	DRIVER'S LICENSE: DATE OF BIRTH MO. 6 DAY 25 YR. 75; NUMBER: N/A; STATE: ; ■ MALE ☐ FEMALE
LICENSE PLATE: YEAR: 13; STATE: NT; NUMBER: DGF-459	LICENSE PLATE: YEAR: N/A; STATE: ; NUMBER:
ESTIMATED DAMAGE TO VEHICLE:	ESTIMATED DAMAGE TO VEHICLE: 500
VEHICLE: YEAR: 02; MAKE: Ford; MODEL: Sedan; BODY STYLE: 4-DR; COLOR: Black	VEHICLE: YEAR: 87; MAKE: GM; MODEL: GP7; BODY STYLE: Locomotive; COLOR:
VEHICLE I.D. NO.: (VIN) OK91U22135	VEHICLE I.D. NO.: (VIN) 1563
ODOMETER READING: Unknown	ODOMETER READING:
OWNER: (Print or Type Full Name) SAME	OWNER: (Print or Type Full Name) Nita & Western Railroad
PHONE:	PHONE:
OWNER'S ADDRESS: (Street or R.F.D.) SAME	OWNER'S ADDRESS: (Street or R.F.D.)
CITY, STATE AND ZIP CODE:	CITY, STATE AND ZIP CODE: Nita City, NT

RESTRAINT INFORMATION — FOR ALL OCCUPANTS IN ALL ACCIDENTS MARK THE APPROPRIATE RESTRAINT CODE IN THE CORRESPONDING SEATING POSITION

VEHICLE-1	VEHICLE-2
Seating position code: 7	N/A
1. Not available 2. Lap belt 3. Lap and shoulder 4. Child restraint 5. Passive restraint 6. Not in use 7. Unknown	1. Not available 2. Lap belt 3. Lap and shoulder 4. Child restraint 5. Passive restraint 6. Not in use 7. Unknown
MOTORCYCLE HELMET: Driver Y ☐ N ☐; Passenger Y ☐ N ☐	MOTORCYCLE HELMET: Driver Y ☐ N ☐; Passenger Y ☐ N ☐

THIS SECTION IS FOR INFORMATION ON INJURED PERSONS ONLY

NAME: Johnny Fitzgerald	AGE: 25
ADDRESS: 16 Meadowbrook Wellington, NT	VEHICLE NUMBER: 1
INJURIES: Crushed Skull	SEX: 1 ■ Male 2 ☐ Female 3 ☐ Unknown
TAKEN TO: Erickson's Mortuary	DARKEN APPROPRIATE SEATING POSITION: 3 6 9 / 2 5 8 / 1 4 7 (4 darkened); K ☐ Pedalcycle L ☐ Moped M ☐ Motorcycle operator N ☐ Motorcycle passenger P ☐ Pedestrian O ☐ Other U ☐ Unknown
BY WHOM: Erickson's Mortuary	EJECTION: 1 ■ Yes 2 ☐ Partial 3 ☐ Unknown 4 ☐ No 5 ☐ Trapped
	TYPE OF INJURY: 1 ☐ Possible injury 2 ☐ Non-incapacitating 3 ☐ Incapacitating 4 ■ Fatal injury

NAME:	AGE:
ADDRESS:	VEHICLE NUMBER:
INJURIES:	SEX: 1 ☐ Male 2 ☐ Female 3 ☐ Unknown
TAKEN TO:	DARKEN APPROPRIATE SEATING POSITION: 3 6 9 / 2 5 8 / 1 4 7; K ☐ Pedalcycle L ☐ Moped M ☐ Motorcycle operator N ☐ Motorcycle passenger P ☐ Pedestrian O ☐ Other U ☐ Unknown
BY WHOM:	EJECTION: 1 ☐ Yes 2 ☐ Partial 3 ☐ Unknown 4 ☐ No 5 ☐ Trapped
	TYPE OF INJURY: 1 ☐ Possible injury 2 ☐ Non-incapacitating 3 ☐ Incapacitating 4 ☐ Fatal injury

NAME:	AGE:
ADDRESS:	VEHICLE NUMBER:
INJURIES:	SEX: 1 ☐ Male 2 ☐ Female 3 ☐ Unknown
TAKEN TO:	DARKEN APPROPRIATE SEATING POSITION: 3 6 9 / 2 5 8 / 1 4 7; K ☐ Pedalcycle L ☐ Moped M ☐ Motorcycle operator N ☐ Motorcycle passenger P ☐ Pedestrian O ☐ Other U ☐ Unknown
BY WHOM:	EJECTION: 1 ☐ Yes 2 ☐ Partial 3 ☐ Unknown 4 ☐ No 5 ☐ Trapped
	TYPE OF INJURY: 1 ☐ Possible injury 2 ☐ Non-incapacitating 3 ☐ Incapacitating 4 ☐ Fatal injury

PROPERTY

STATE OBJECT & NATURE OF DAMAGE, OTHER THAN VEHICLE:		APPROXIMATE COST OF DAMAGE: $
OWNER: (Name)	ADDRESS:	PHONE:

WITNESSES

NAME	ADDRESS		PHONE
Rich April	Route 7	Nita CIty, NT	
Matt Green	716 Main	Nita City, NT	
Stacy Beck	Route 8	Wellington, NT	

DR Form 40, Nov 84 — THIS FORM REPLACES DR FORM 40, JUNE 78. PREVIOUS EDITIONS WILL BE DESTROYED. — 1810

JX 19

Vehicle Accident Report

THE FOLLOWING INFORMATION IS REQUIRED FOR ALL ACCIDENTS

DRIVER AND VEHICLE INFORMATION

VEHICLE MOVEMENT BEFORE COLLISION

	N	S	E	W	ROAD OR HIGHWAY NAME
1			[x]		County Rd
2	[x]				RR TRacks

VEH 1 2
- 1 [x] [x] Going ahead
- 2 [ ] [ ] Passing
- 3 [ ] [ ] Turning right
- 4 [ ] [ ] Turning left
- 5 [ ] [ ] Making "U" turn
- 6 [ ] [ ] Slowing down
- 7 [ ] [ ] Starting in traffic lane
- 8 [ ] [ ] Starting from parked position
- 9 [ ] [ ] Backing up
- 10 [ ] [ ] Stopped in traffic lane
- 11 [ ] [ ] Parked
- 12 [ ] [ ] Merging
- 13 [ ] [ ] Changing lanes

DISPOSITION OF VEHICLE *(Check one per vehicle)*

VEH 1 2
- 1 [x] [ ] Towed away
- 2 [ ] [ ] Abandoned
- 3 [ ] [x] Driven away
- 4 [ ] [ ] Unknown

VEHICLE - 1

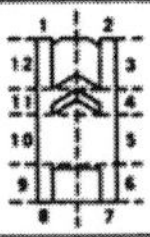

- 13 [ ] TOP
- 14 [ ] BOTTOM
- 15 [x] TOTAL
- 16 [ ] UNKNOWN

VEHICLE - 2

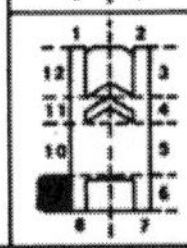

- 13 [ ] TOP
- 14 [ ] BOTTOM
- 15 [ ] TOTAL
- 16 [ ] UNKNOWN

VEHICLE CONDITION *(Check one per vehicle)*

VEH 1 2
- 1 [ ] [ ] No defects
- 2 [ ] [ ] Defective Brakes
- 3 [ ] [ ] Defective lights
- 4 [ ] [ ] Defective signals
- 5 [ ] [ ] Defective steering
- 6 [ ] [ ] Defective tires
- 7 [x] [x] Unknown
- 8 [ ] [ ] Other *(Specify)*

MAJOR CONTRIBUTING CIRCUMSTANCES *(Check one per accident)*

VEH 1 2
- 1 [ ] [ ] Speed too fast for conditions
- 2 [ ] [ ] Exceeding speed limit
- 3 [ ] [ ] Alcohol or drugs
- 4 [ ] [ ] Failure to yield
- 5 [ ] [ ] Drove left of center
- 6 [ ] [ ] Improper overtaking
- 7 [ ] [ ] Ran stop sign
- 8 [ ] [ ] Disregarded traffic signal
- 9 [ ] [ ] Following too closely
- 10 [ ] [ ] Following too closely
- 11 [ ] [ ] Made improper turn
- 12 [ ] [ ] Improper or no turn signal
- 15 [ ] [ ] Evasive action
- 16 [ ] [ ] Backing unsafely
- 18 [x] [ ] Other *(Specify below)*
- 19 [ ] [ ] Improper lane change
- 20 [ ] [ ] Animal on roadway

Inattentiveness

MAJOR REASON FOR NOT SEEING DANGER *(Check one per vehicle)*

VEH 1 2
- 1 [ ] [ ] None
- 2 [ ] [ ] Rain, snow, ice on windshield
- 3 [ ] [ ] Dirty windshield
- 4 [ ] [ ] Trees, crops, etc.
- 5 [ ] [ ] Buildings
- 6 [ ] [ ] Embankment
- 7 [ ] [ ] Traffic sign
- 8 [ ] [ ] Billboard
- 9 [ ] [ ] Parked vehicle
- 10 [ ] [ ] Moving vehicle
- 11 [x] [x] Other *(Specify)*

DRIVER'S CONDITION *(Check one per vehicle)*

VEH 1 2
- 1 [x] [x] Normal
- 2 [ ] [ ] Asleep
- 3 [ ] [ ] Illness
- 4 [ ] [ ] Fatigue
- 5 [ ] [ ] Drinking
- 6 [ ] [ ] Unknown
- 7 [ ] [ ] Other *(Specify)*

PEDESTRIAN'S CONDITION *(Check one)*

- 1 [ ] Normal
- 2 [ ] Asleep
- 3 [ ] Illness
- 4 [ ] Fatigue
- 5 [ ] Drinking
- 6 [ ] Unknown
- 7 [ ] Other *(Specify)*

ACCIDENT INFORMATION

ROAD CHARACTER *(Check one)*

- 1 [ ] Straight and level
- 2 [x] Straight and on grade
- 3 [ ] Straight and at hillcrest
- 4 [ ] Curved and level
- 5 [ ] Curved and on grade
- 6 [ ] Curved and on hillcrest

ROAD TYPE *(Check one)*

- 1 [ ] One lane
- 2 [x] Two lanes
- 3 [ ] Three lanes
- 4 [ ] Four or more lanes
- 5 [ ] Divided roadway
- 6 [ ] Interstate

ROAD SURFACE *(Check one)*

- 1 [ ] Concrete
- 2 [ ] Black top
- 3 [ ] Brick
- 4 [x] Gravel
- 5 [ ] Dirt
- 6 [ ] Other *(Specify)*

ROAD SURFACE CONDITION *(Check one)*

- 1 [x] Dry
- 2 [ ] Wet
- 3 [ ] Snowy - icy
- 4 [ ] Other *(Specify)*

WEATHER *(Check one)*

- 1 [x] Clear
- 2 [ ] Raining
- 3 [ ] Snowing
- 4 [ ] Fog
- 5 [ ] Cloudy
- 6 [ ] Other *(Specify)*

Temperature ______

ROAD WORK *(Check one)*

- 1 [ ] Construction zone
- 2 [ ] Maintenance activity
- 3 [ ] Not applicable

TRAFFIC CONTROL *(Check up to two)*

- 1 [ ] None
- 2 [ ] Stop sign
- 3 [ ] Yield sign
- 4 [ ] Traffic signal
- 5 [ ] Pedestrian signal
- 6 [ ] Pedestrian crosswalk
- 7 [ ] Flashing beacon
- 8 [ ] Railroad warning sign
- 9 [x] Railroad crossing sign
- 10 [ ] Railroad flashing beacon
- 11 [ ] Railroad gates & signal
- 13 [ ] Officer/flagman
- 14 [ ] No passing zone *(signs)*
- 15 [ ] No passing zone *(paint stripes)*
- 16 [ ] Other *(Specify)*

LIGHT CONDITION *(Check one)*

- 1 [x] Daylight
- 2 [ ] Dawn - dusk
- 3 [ ] Darkness
- 4 [ ] Darkness - streetlights on
- 5 [ ] Darkness - streetlights off

PEDESTRIAN'S ACTION *(Check one)*

- 1 [ ] Crossing at intersection - with signal
- 2 [ ] Crossing at intersection - against signal
- 3 [ ] Crossing at intersection - no signal
- 4 [ ] Crossing - not at intersection
- 5 [ ] Walking with traffic
- 6 [ ] Walking against traffic
- 7 [ ] Standing in roadway
- 8 [ ] Getting on or off other vehicle
- 9 [ ] Working on vehicle on roadway
- 10 [ ] Other working in roadway
- 11 [ ] Playing in roadway
- 12 [ ] Other in roadway
- 13 [ ] Not in roadway
- 14 [ ] Other *(Specify)*

INDICATE BY DIAGRAM WHAT HAPPENED

See Attached Diagrams

N

Narrative: Vehicle #1 was eastbound on County Road when it collided with rear of first box car on freight train. Vehicle #1 apparently struck box car #1 just in front of rear wheels and was dragged by train along tracks. Box car #1 ran over vehicle #1, causing back wheels to derail and break coupling between box car #1 and box car #2. Train continued along tracks with rear section stopping, Vehicle #1 being pulled along and then stopping, then front part of train stopping. No vissible signs of skid marks at scene, only scuff marks at collision site. Conclusion that there was no attempt to stop Vehicle #1. **No visible confirmation of seat belt use. Airbag deployed. D1 ejected.**

Engineer of train said "We were northbound and unaware of anything until the train went into emergency." Mark Edwards, investigator for railroad, advised that speed tape in engine showed train was traveling at 48 mph at time of accident. Train consisted of four engines and 85 cars (24 loaded, 61 empty) with total weight of 4033 tons. Crossing protected by one crossbuck sign facing eastbound on north side of road.

Inattentiveness was probably the major cause of the accident.

DESCRIBE BELOW WHAT HAPPENED: *(Refer to vehicle by number)*

Should location have engineering study	Were photographs taken	Was investigation made at scene	Is investigation complete	Driver report form furnished to
[ ] YES [x] NO	[x] YES [ ] NO	[x] YES [ ] NO	[x] YES [ ] NO	[ ] 1 [ ] 2

INVESTIGATOR'S RANK & WRITTEN SIGNATURE:	DEPARTMENT:	OFFICER NO.:	TROOP:	MO.	DAY	YR.
Michael Benjamin, Trooper	Nita State Police	122	C	10	22	13

MAIL TO: ACCIDENT RECORDS BUREAU, DEPARTMENT OF ROADS

JX 20

Vehicle Accident Report

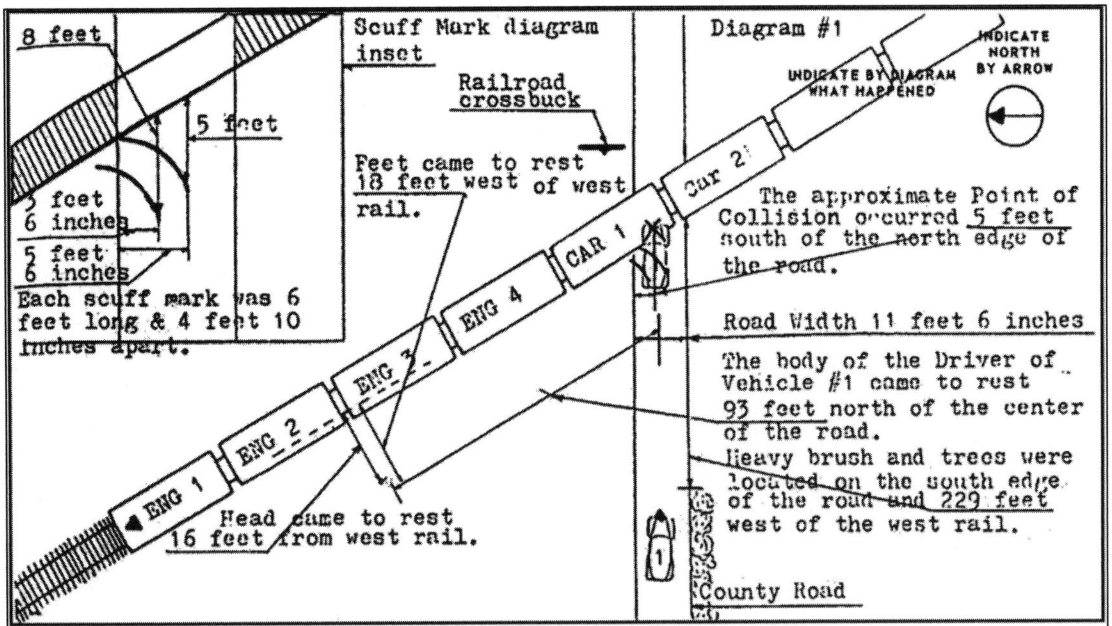

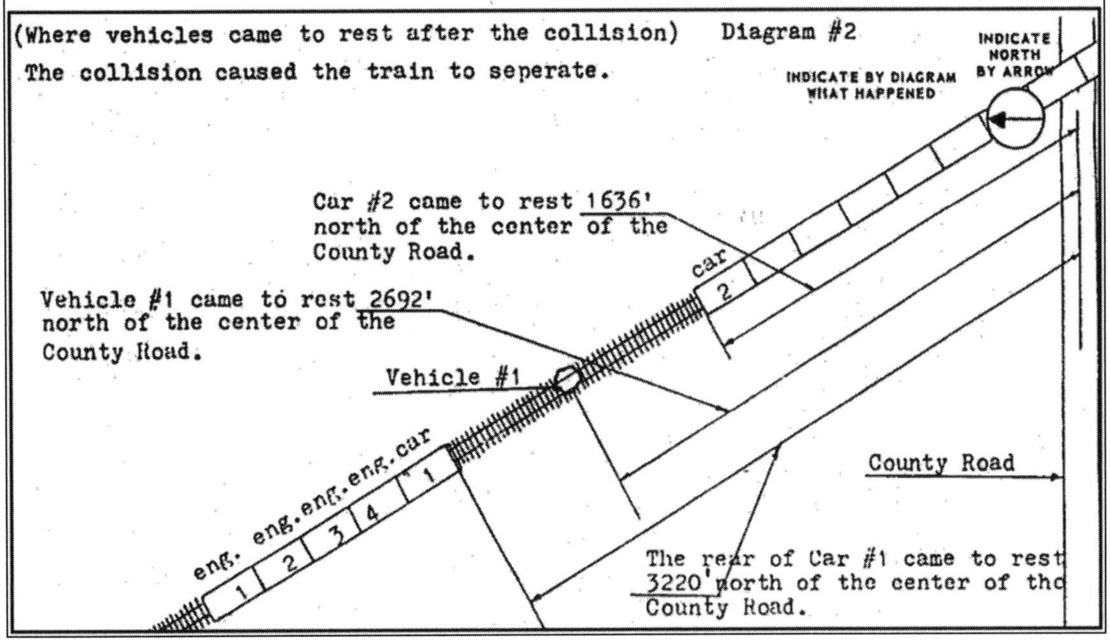

JX 21

Vehicle Accident Report

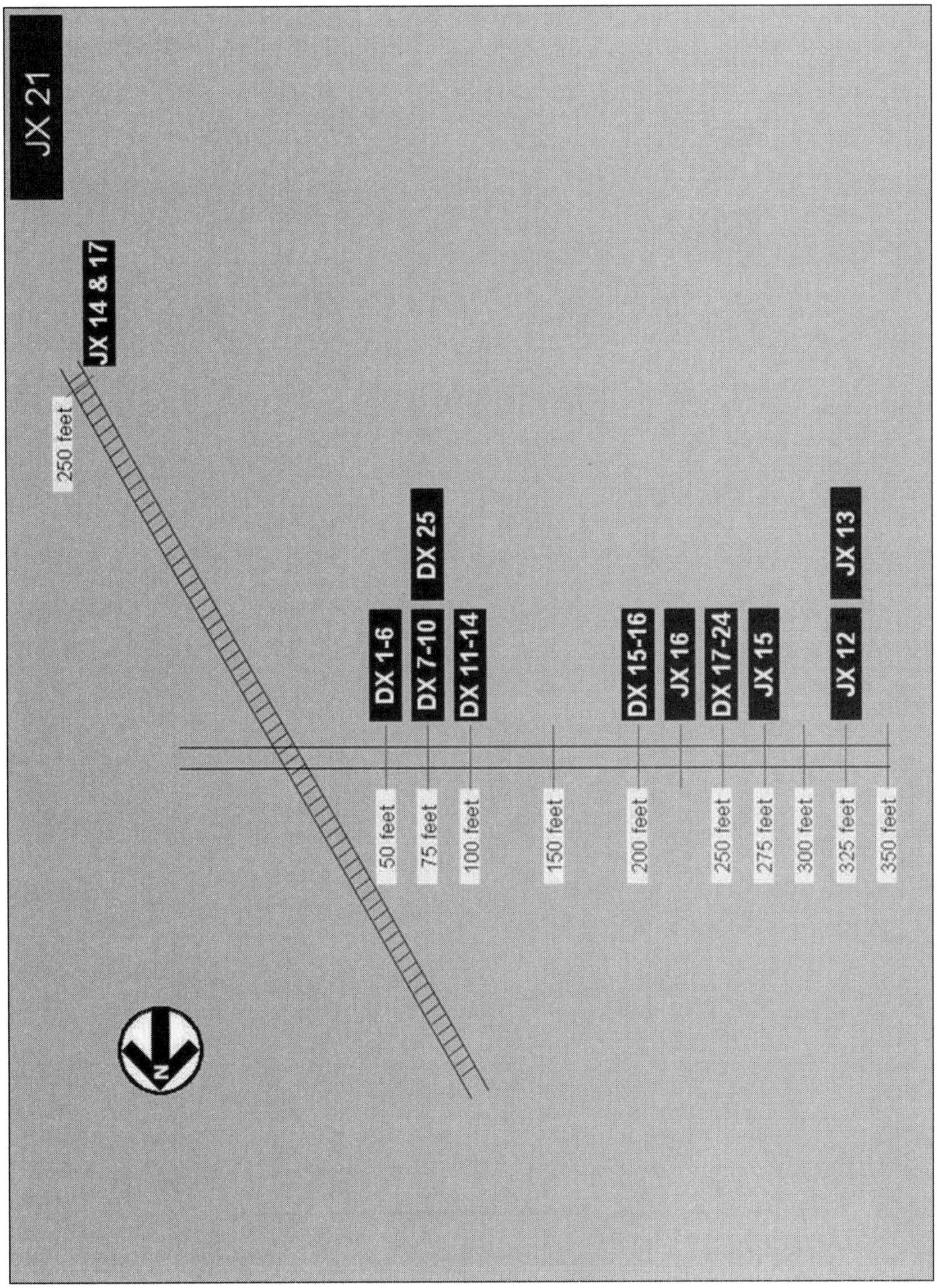

Email from Paralegal Alex Emerson to Plaintiffs' Attorney Busch

To: Tom Busch <TBuschAtty@Busch&Associates.nita>

From: Alex Emerson <AEmerson1@Busch&Associates.nita>

Date: 19 Jan 2014 14:36

Subject: Fitzgerald v. Nita & Western Railroad

Attach//: FitzvN&WRR/Photos/AEmerson

At your request, today I interviewed State Trooper Mike Benjamin regarding his investigation of the accident involving our client's husband, Johnny Fitzgerald, and the Nita & Western freight train on October 20, 2013. I was especially concerned about the description of the photographs he took. The substance of the interview follows.

Trooper Mike Benjamin, DOB 1/22/1990, is a graduate of Lisle High School and received an associate degree in administration of criminal justice from Columbia County Community College in 2010. He then joined the Nita State Police. In connection with his training as a trooper, he has attended the State Police Training Academy in Nita City for two months, including a two-week session on accident investigation, as well as another two-week session put on by the Northwestern Traffic Institute in Evanston, Illinois. Over the last three years, he has investigated over 500 automobile accidents, but this was the first auto-train collision he has investigated.

He was on routine patrol on Sunday, October 20, 2013, when he received a call to report to County Road at the railroad crossing to investigate an accident. He approached the intersection from the west and did not observe any advance warning sign that a railroad crossing was coming up, and he commented that the foliage along the road was heavy. He arrived at the scene at about 6:00 p.m. and found the train in two sections and the railroad employees examining the train. One of the railroad men indicated that he had found a man up the tracks, and Benjamin went to the location. He found Mr. Fitzgerald, determined that he was dead, and observed that Mr. Fitzgerald had suffered a crushed skull. He covered the body and then radioed to cancel the ambulance and request the mortuary/coroner to come out. He spoke to the railroad investigator, Mark Edwards, who arrived shortly thereafter and began taking measurements with the aid of a passerby. He took the names of the railroad witnesses as well as the neighbor who was on the scene. The neighbor told him that he had called the police but had not been an eyewitness.

He told me that he noticed two definite scuff marks near the tracks just west of the rails that were fresh. He was unable to say on the basis of the physical evidence exactly where the train had been separated. However, he was fairly confident that it had separated as a result of going over the car that it had dragged.

He also confirmed that there was only one crossbuck and that it was facing east with lettering on the east side. He also said that it was in disrepair in that one of the cross pieces was broken.

He took two sets of photographs. The first set (photos 1–5) was at about 6:25 in the evening the night of the accident, just at sunset. The second set (photos 6–17) was taken the following day at about 2:30 p.m. He is not very familiar with the crossing and could not comment about any level of traffic across the tracks, nor of any recent increases. I have attached copies of these photos to this email so you can view them at your convenience.

> Photo 1 shows the grooves from the rear wheels of the Fitzgerald car and its relationship to the tracks. Also shown is the box car that stopped at the crossing.
>
> Photo 2 shows the front section of the train with the derailed wheels on box car No. 1 and the four engines. It was taken from east of the tracks looking northwesterly.
>
> Photo 3 is of box car No. 1 and the front of the train. Clearly shown are the scrape marks on the rear portion of box car No. 1 where the car impacted.
>
> Photo 4 shows the derailed wheels on box car No. 1.
>
> Photo 5 shows the Fitzgerald car where it came to rest.

All of the remaining photos were taken the next day.

> Photo 6 was taken from the top of the hill west of the crossing, looking east. It is the beginning of a steep incline, and the tracks are pictured in the distance.
>
> Photo 7 is going down the incline with the tracks still visible.
>
> Photo 8 is farther down the road with the tracks no longer visible.
>
> Photo 9 is yet farther down the road; the tracks are still not visible.
>
> Photo 10 is again down the road.
>
> Photo 11 is at the bottom of the incline.
>
> Photo 12 is at a point 325 feet west of the crossing looking east toward the tracks, which now become visible.
>
> Photo 13 is from the 325-foot point and looking through the brush and trees toward the southwest where the train was coming from; it was taken at eye level from inside the trooper's car.
>
> Photo 14 is taken from a point 250 feet south of the crossing down the tracks looking northwest to the point where the car is 325 feet up the road; the car is barely visible.

Photo 15 is again looking east from the road at the 275-foot mark; the crossbuck is barely visible.

Photo 16 is looking east at the 225-foot mark; the crossbuck is now clearly visible.

Photo 17 is from the previously noted point on the tracks (250 feet south of the center line of the street) looking northwest, with the car at the 225-foot mark.

Trooper Benjamin was also clear that it was the railroad's obligation to keep the brush down along the road for a reasonable distance. Although the roadside foliage had blocked Fitzgerald's view of the train, Benjamin felt that the whistle should have warned him of the oncoming train. While Fitzgerald was in the darkness of the foliage and broke out into the light, Benjamin felt that there was still enough time to see the train and stop. He was apparently unaware that the whistle was not sounding, and I did not mention this fact to him.

I asked him if he had any theory on why there were no skid marks. He indicated that there could only be two causes: intentional and unintentional. If it was unintentional, it was the result of inattention or a malfunction of the car. If it was intentional, he either committed suicide or Fitzgerald tried to beat the train across the crossing. I also asked him about the seatbelt. He told me that he could not tell whether the belt was used or not, as it was not latched when he saw it, but it could have become unlatched by the collision. He will make a convincing witness as to the photos, although we must counter his conclusion as to the inattentiveness of our decedent.

Alex

Alex Emerson
Paralegal Busch & Associates
(555) 264-4822, ext. 112, Fax (555) 265-4823

JX 1

Trooper Photo 1

JX 2

Trooper Photo 2

JX 3

Trooper Photo 3

JX 4

Trooper Photo 4

JX 5

Trooper Photo 5

JX 6

Trooper Photo 6

JX 7

Trooper Photo 7

JX 8

Trooper Photo 8

JX 9

Trooper Photo 9

JX 10

Trooper Photo 10

JX 11

Trooper Photo 11

JX 12

Trooper Photo 12

JX 13

Trooper Photo 13

JX 14

Trooper Photo 14

JX 15

Trooper Photo 15

JX 16

Trooper Photo 16

JX 17

Trooper Photo 17

PX 4

David Jonathan & Associates, Inc.

Consultants in Railroad Safety and Engineering
19 Erin Marie Court
Nita City, Nita 49099
(555) 264-6593 Fax (555) 264-6594
djonathan@dja.nita

October 30, 2014

Thomas Busch, Esq.
Busch & Associates
2000 Johnson Drive
Wellington, Nita

RE: Nita & Western Railroad Crossing #74647C
County Road
Wellington, Nita

Dear Mr. Busch:

In accordance with your request, I have conducted an examination concerning the above crossing and the accident of October 20, 2013. Based upon my investigation, it is my opinion that Nita & Western Railroad was negligent in the following ways:

1. Failure to timely upgrade the crossing to include flashing signals and audible warnings;

2. Failure of the engineer to sound whistles to warn nearby traffic;

3. Failure to maintain the foliage along an intersecting roadway.

In connection with my investigation, I have examined the following documents:

1. State police report concerning the accident, with photos, dated October 22, 2013;

2. Available maps;

3. Statement of Stacy Beck, November 23, 2013;

4. Report of Mark Edwards, Investigator for Nita & Western Railroad, with photographs, dated October 26, 2013;

5. Letter to you from Nita Highway and Transportation Commission, dated September 30, 2014, with attached hourly traffic count for period February 26 to March 4, 2013;

6. Letter to you from Douglas County Highway Department, dated September 22, 2014;

7. Letter to John Colton, Esq., from Dr. Joshua Alan, dated May 21, 2014.

In addition, I visited the actual crossing on two occasions. The first was on August 1, 2014, and the second was on October 24, 2014, four days after the first anniversary of the accident.

Although the history of this crossing shows only one automobile-train accident during the last twenty-five years, the increased traffic resulting from the establishment of the new Uprite Scaffolding plant (occupied September 2012) leads me to conclude, in my expert opinion, that automatic flashing/sounding signals should have been installed long before this accident. In fact, they should have been installed as soon as a full crew was operating to build the plant. The entire time I was with Louisville & Nashville and Union Pacific, the standard procedure at those railroads and in the industry today is that as soon as the state highway commission puts a crossing on an eligibility list for flashing light signals, within two weeks the railroad's engineering crew would do a feasibility study on whether automatic signals should be installed at that crossing. Included in this feasibility study would not only be a study of present traffic conditions, but also a study of conditions that could be anticipated in the following six months based on local construction or predictable traffic patterns. Based on the data supplied by the state that this crossing was placed on an eligibility list in March 2013 and the fact that the traffic to the plant was increasing, Nita & Western was negligent in either not doing the study or in not installing the automatic crossing signals called for by the study within a timely manner. Doing a feasibility study eleven months after placement on the eligibility list and installation of flashing lights seventeen months after the placement are both acts of negligence, although taking six months for the installation is reasonable.

Because I have worked in railroads for almost forty-five years, I am well aware of standard railroad regulations regarding requirements for headlamps and whistles. By state law and railroad regulations, whistles must be sounded at least 1,200 feet in advance of a railroad crossing. This is a necessary safety procedure, which if not followed would make it materially more difficult for an automobile driver to hear a train approaching a crossing. In my expert opinion, having examined the scene and the photographs taken on the day of the accident, if the whistle was not sounding, it would be extremely difficult for Mr. Fitzgerald, in diminishing daylight and breaking out of an area of dense foliage, to recognize that a train was approaching or at the crossing.

As to the extent of the foliage, I believe that the railroad could certainly have made clearer the approach to the intersection. I would suggest, based upon the speed limit of the road, that all dense foliage should have been cleared 350 feet from the crossing.

Furthermore, I agree with Dr. Joshua Alan that the marks at the crossing were not skid marks, but were caused by the train pulling the car. Accordingly, it is apparent that Mr. Fitzgerald was not alerted by any sound or light. Therefore, in my opinion, the whistle was not sounding before the collision.

To date I have spent eight hours on this matter. Accordingly, please treat this letter as an invoice for $2,800. Should you require my services for a deposition or for in-court testimony, please advise me as soon as possible so that no scheduling conflicts arise.

Very truly yours,

David Jonathan

David Jonathan, President
David Jonathan & Associates, Inc.

DJ/kp
enc.

PX 5

David Jonathan

19 Erin Marie Court
Nita City, Nita 49099
Home (515) 264-1159
Cell phone (515) 265-3088
djonathan@dja.nita

Education

May 1970	BS, Civil Engineering University of Nita

Employment

2010 to Present	President, David Jonathan & Associates, Inc. Consultants specializing in railroad safety and engineering
1978 to 2010	Chief Civil Engineer, Union Pacific Railroad
1970 to 1978	Staff Engineer, Louisville & Nashville Railroad

Expert Witness Experience

Testimony for both plaintiffs and defendants

Qualified as an expert in four federal and three state courts

Testified in court in twelve cases on:

- crossing safety
- operations safety
- civil engineering

Fees:

- $350 per hour for investigation and report
- $350 per hour for deposition preparation/testimony
- $300 per hour for in-court preparation/testimony
- Reimbursement of all necessary expenses

PX 6

Committed to recycling to keep Nita transportation routes beautiful

Theresa DeSalvo, Chair

State of Nita

Highway and Transportation Commission
State Office Building
Nita City, Nita
(515) 264-1010
htcommission@state.nita

September 30, 2014

Thomas Busch, Esq.
Busch & Associates
2000 Johnson Drive
Wellington, Nita

Re: Nita & Western Crossing #74647C
County Road
Wellington, Nita

Dear Mr. Busch:

Reference is made to your letter of September 2, 2014, concerning the subject crossing. A review of our files indicates that only one vehicle count was taken at this location during the last five years. A copy of the summary sheet for the count, which occurred from February 26 to March 4, 2013, is enclosed.

Regarding your request for a priority list, please be advised that we have an ongoing program to upgrade railroad crossings. In conjunction with this program, we develop a number of eligibility listings that are constantly changing as conditions in the field change. Once a crossing appears on an eligibility listing, the railroad is required within a reasonable time to do a feasibility study to determine what, if any, crossing upgrade work is merited. The crossing in question first appeared on an eligibility listing in March 2013. Our records show that a feasibility study was done by Nita & Western in February 2014 and that flashing light signals were installed at the crossing in August of 2014.

If we may be of any additional assistance, please advise.

Very truly yours,

Cory Nathan

Corey Nathan

PX 6

Vehicle Count Summary

Location Number: 861 Direction: Both Year: 2013

Crossing No.: 74647C Location: County Road County: Douglas

Railroad: Nita & Western Period: Feb. 26, 10:30 a.m. through March 4, 8:30 a.m.

	Thur Feb 26		Fri Feb 27		Sat Feb 28	
	a.m.	p.m.	a.m.	p.m.	a.m.	p.m.
1		26	6	24	15	32
2		13	4	21	10	28
3		38	2	41	1	28
4		54		50	1	48
5		88	5	74	2	33
6		74	16	59	2	24
7		41	47	55	17	37
8		26	61	33	17	24
9		17	35	20	25	25
10		18	16	19	31	16
11		12	13	18	46	9
12	28	7	26	21	41	7

PX 6

Vehicle Count Summary

	Sun Mar 1		Mon Mar 2		Tues Mar 3		Wed Mar 4	
	a.m.	p.m.	a.m.	p.m.	a.m.	p.m.	a.m.	p.m.
1	17	38	2	24	7	24	8	
2	7	24		11	2	18	2	
3	8	32		18	2	29	3	
4	3	49	1	42	1	51		
5	2	44	1	78	3	74	3	
6	1	23	12	56	13	58	15	
7	2	32	41	92	43	46	40	
8	3	19	52	24	50	27	51	
9	12	17	20	19	20	11	33	
10	37	13	23	17	22	20		
11	26	11	23	17	10	10		
12	28	6	10	9	22	8		

Totals	Date	24 Hours	Avg./hr	6 a.m.-10	Avg./hr
Thur	Feb 26	647	26.958	405	36.818
Fri	Feb 27	666	27.750	591	53.727
Sat	Feb 28	519	21.625	458	41.636
Sun	Mar 1	444	18.500	387	35.181
Mon	Mar 2	592	24.667	545	49.545
Tue	Mar 3	571	23.792	518	47.091
Wed	Mar 4	155	6.458	124	11.272

PX 7

Douglas County
State of Nita

Highway Department
205 North Second Street
Wellington, Nita

(515) 267-4111 Fax: (515) 267-4112 Email: Doughway@county.nita

September 22, 2014

Thomas Busch, Esq.
Busch & Associates
2000 Johnson Drive
Wellington, Nita

RE: Nita & Western Railroad Crossing #74647C
County Road
Wellington, Nita

Dear Mr. Busch:

In response to your letter of September 2, 2014, requesting traffic counts at the crossing referred above, the following is the traffic count information we have available.

2013 traffic count by the State of Nita—average daily traffic: 620.

Traffic count by Douglas County in March/April 2014—average daily traffic: 1,089.

I hope that the above information is useful.

Sincerely,

Stanley Davis

County Highway Engineer

PX 8

University of Nita

William F. Landsea, PhD
Forensic Economist
Professor of Economics
University of Nita
Nita City, Nita 49099
Wlandsea@gmail.nita

Thomas Busch, Esq.
Busch & Associates
2000 Johnson Drive
Wellington, Nita

Sept. 22, 2014

Re: Economic Damages, Johnny Fitzgerald

Dear Mr. Busch:

At your request, I have calculated economic damage suffered by the dependent family and estate of Mr. Johnny Fitzgerald as a consequence of his untimely death in a car-train accident on October 20, 2013. At the date of his death, that family consisted of Mrs. Debra Fitzgerald, age 23, and daughter Natalie, age 5. Economic damage calculations assumed that Mr. Fitzgerald would otherwise have lived a normal life expectancy to age 79 and would have been employed through a normal worklife to age 65. Damage calculations also assumed that Mr. Fitzgerald would have provided household services to his wife and daughter to the end of his normal life expectancy. The analysis of economic damages is predicated upon material facts and opinions documented in my files. The analysis of economic damages was performed using standard damage models, incorporating generally accepted present-value methodology.

I find that Mr. Fitzgerald's dependent family and estate have suffered economic damages with the present values shown below. Present value is the amount necessary now that with interest at the stated rate (3.3 percent tax-free) would exactly compensate in a timely fashion the economic values lost by his untimely death. Present value does not include any prejudgment interest amounts on past damages.

Lost Past and Future Household Services:	$3,359,757
Lost Past and Future Financial Support:	$1,125,034
Lost Net Estate Accumulations	$48,259
Total Present Value, Calculated Economic Damages:	$4,533,050

Mr. Fitzgerald's income earning potential was projected based upon United States Department of Labor information regarding incomes normally earned by welders, his occupation at the time of death. These would provide an annual income of $42,900 before taxes and benefits. Mr. Fitzgerald's own tax returns showed earned income in the range of $39,789 to $43,911 in the three full years preceding his death. Adjusting the projected income for benefits (12 %), income tax (5%), and his own anticipated expenditures (28%) and normal savings (5%) leaves a balance of $31,746 projected as normally available for financial support of his dependent family. These were projected forward including increases for anticipated cost of living (inflationary) increases (2.0 percent), productivity changes (0.5 percent). They were calculated to the end of a normal work life at age 65 consistent with United States Department of Labor projections.

The other element of damage is the loss of services normally rendered by Mr. Fitzgerald to members of his household. The survivors identified various active services (basically household chores) that Mr. Fitzgerald performed on the average about two hours a day. This is quite consistent with findings reported in the authoritative United States Department of Labor's "American Time Use Survey" for active services performed in the household by adult males. Valuing these at a market (replacement) cost of $13 per hour indicates that active services worth $9,464 annually have been lost to the family. As with his wages, these costs were projected to increase in the future by cost of living and productivity changes.

In addition to active services lost, calculations of lost passive services were also provided. These necessary services are provided in a mostly passive manner—including some provided while the service provider is sleeping. They include security, protection, and stand-by for active care when needed. Passive service hours are measured as time spent with family members net of the active service hours. In a week, passive service would approximate 94 hours after accounting for 60 hours a week away from the home and family for work, commuting, and other personal time use and after the 14 hours spent on the active services that are accounted for separately. Valuing the replacement cost again at $13 per hour indicates an annual loss to family members of $63,544.

The third element of economic loss addressed here is the loss of net estate accumulations. This loss to the estate arises when the untimely death of Mr. Fitzgerald interrupts his normal pattern of saving and accumulation of assets that become his final estate. Data from the Consumer Expenditure Survey (Bureau of Labor Statistics, United States Department of Labor) show that earners with incomes near Mr. Fitzgerald's will save approximately 5% per year of their incomes. The calculations of loss here assume Mr. Fitzgerald would have done that to a normal worklife and that once saved interest at the 3.3% discount rate would be earned on the accumulating balance. At age 79, the normal life expectancy, that estate amount would have accumulated to $131,221, the present value of which today is $48,259.

All economic factors and opinions underlying the projection of lost financial support, lost household services, and lost net estate accumulations are shown on the economic damages worksheets accompanying this report. The worksheets illustrate the process of projecting damages annually and show the reduction to present value amounts by the year and in total.

Damages by funeral and final medical expenses are a matter of record, not normally an economic projection, and were therefore not included in the economic damage calculations reported here.

Economic damage opinions reported here are based upon currently available information and are valued as of the current date. They are subject to change with new information and/or the passing of time.

My time to date totals 23.5 hours. This will be billed at my standard pretrial rate of $485 per hour. I have no other interest in the case, its outcome, or the principals. Lastly, I have attached a copy of my professional resume.

Respectively yours,

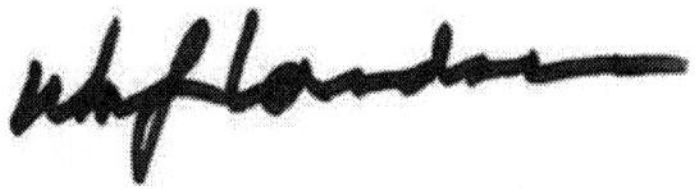

William F. Landsea, PhD

Consulting Forensic Economist

WFL/lot

Enclosure

PX 9

William F. Landsea, PhD

Consulting Forensic Economist

Notice and Mailing Address:

15620 S.W. 77th. Avenue, Nita City, Nita 49049

Email: Wlandsea@gmail.nita

Phones:

Home Office: 515-969-8844

Fax: 515-969-8855

Cell: 515-323-3618

Education:

BS Urban Land Economics, University of Illinois, 1961; MS Finance, University of Illinois, 1964; PhD Finance, University of Illinois, 1966

Experience:

Instructor, University of Illinois, 1963–1965

Assistant Professor and Associate Professor, University of Miami, 1965–2009

Chairman, Finance Department, University of Miami, 1978

Member of Board, Chicago Heights National Bank, 1970–1971

Member of Board, and Chairman, University Credit Union 1966–1987

Guest Lecturer, School of Law, University of Miami, 1993–1999

Consultant: Economic and real estate consultant to attorneys, investors, and developers business organizations, financial institutions, municipalities, and community development agencies.

Expert Witness: Economic damages: personal injury, wrongful death, real estate, stigma, eminent domain, ad valorem, and business losses and valuations.

Vice President AAEFE and Member Board of Editors Journal of Legal Economics.

President, 2008–2009, Collegium of Pecuniary Damage Experts

Board of Editors, The Earnings Analyst, AREA and CPDE

Professional Memberships:

National Association of Forensic Economists

Southern Finance Association

Southern Economic Association

Real Estate Educators Association

National Association of Business Economists, 1990 to date

American Rehabilitation Economics Association (AREA)

American Law and Economics Association

American Academy of Economic and Financial Experts, 1994 to date

American Real Estate Society

Southwestern Finance Association

Collegium of Pecuniary Damage Experts (CPDE)

Relevant Publications:

"The Outlook for Regional Stock Exchanges," THE SOUTHERN JOURNAL OF BUSINESS, April 1969.

"Agency Bonds in the Liquidity Portfolio," MISSISSIPPI VALLEY JOURNAL OF BUSINESS and ECONOMICS, Vol. V, No. 2, Winter, 71–2.

"Regional Emphasis in Real Estate Syndication," REAL ESTATE SYNDICATION REPORTER.

ANNUAL REPORT, 1979-80, with Seth Werner, pp. 127–132.

THE IMPACT OF CONDOMINIUM CONVERSION, DADE, BROWARD, PALM BEACH AND PINELLAS COUNTIES. 77 pages, with B. Hersker, L.A.Klatt, and M.G. Parsons, 1980, Florida Association of Realtors.

"How Workable Are Net Discount Rates?" McGILL LAW JOURNAL, Vol. 28, No. 1, Dec. 1982, pp. 102–115.

"Inflation and the Present Value of Future Economic Damages," UNIVERSITY OF MIAMI LAW REVIEW. Vol. 37, No. 1, Nov. 1982 with David L. Roberts, pp. 93–122.

"POPULAR SCHEMES FOR REAL ESTATE INVESTING: A RISK ANALYSIS," 1990, 53 pages, Education and Research Foundation, Florida Real Estate Commission.

"Worklife—Definitions and Impact on Methodology," JOURNAL OF LEGAL ECONOMICS, Vol. 1, No. 1, March 1991, pp. 51–62.

"Get Real! A Comment on the Need for 'Adjustments' in Discounting Future Damage Amounts," JOURNAL OF FORENSIC ECONOMICS, Vol. 7, No. 3, pp. 161–162.

"Questionable Reasonableness of Trout and Foster's Method of Estimating a Decedent's Consumption," JOURNAL OF FORENSIC ECONOMICS, Vol. 7 No. 2, p. 211. Reprinted as chapter in ASSESSING FAMILY LOSS IN WRONGFUL DEATH LITIGATION: The Special Roles of Lost Services and Personal Consumption., Ireland and Depperschmidt, Editors, Lawyers and Judges Publishing Co., 1999.

"Projecting the Benefits of Earning Capacity," JOURNAL of LEGAL ECONOMICS, Vol. 4, No. 3, Winter 1994, pp. 73–83.

"There is No Free Lunch: Risky Discount Rates Still Risky," JOURNAL of LEGAL ECONOMICS, Vol. 9, No. 2, Fall 1999, pp. 1–7.

"Earning Capacity, Highest and Best, or Something Else?" With Robert A. Male, THE EARNING ANALYST, Vol. XI, 2010, pp. 22–26.

PX 10

Economic Analysis Report

Johnny Fitzgerald

Fitzgerald v. Nita & Western Railroad

Prepared by

William F. Landsea

Professor of Economics

University of Nita

Nita City, Nita

Sept. 22, 2014

PX 10

SUMMARY OF ECONOMIC DAMAGE CALCULATIONS — VALUES PROJECTED TO NORMAL LIFE EXPECTANCY

JOHNNY FITZGERALD

Category of loss:	Present value of damage: PAST	FUTURE	TOTAL
A. Lost Net Estate Accumulations	na	$48,259	$48,259
B. Lost Financial Support	$29,974	$1,095,061	$1,125,034
C. Lost Services to Household			
1. Active Services	$9,078	$426,446	$435,524
2. Passive Services	$60,949	$2,863,283	$2,924,233
D. Total All Calculated Losses	$100,000	$4,433,050	$4,533,050

This summary sheet must be accompanied by related damage worksheets illustrating calculation of damage amounts and stating underlying economic factors. Damage amounts valid as of Sept. 14, 2014

prepared by: William F. Landsea, Ph.D. printed on: 11/25/14

PX 10

LOST FINANCIAL SUPPORT AND ESTATE ACCUMULATIONS
JOHNNY FITZGERALD

page 1

Economic Factors Re:	JOHNNY FITZGERALD			
1	Date of analysis, years since d/d:	9/30/2014		0.94
2	Date of birth, current age would be:	10/24/89		24.93
3	Date of death (d/d) at age:	10/20/13		23.99
4	Normal Life Expectancy to Age (1):			79 years
5	Normal Worklife Expectancy (12)			to age 65
6	Household Members:		Born	current age
7	Wife, Debra Fitzgerald		4/6/1990	24.48
8	Normal Life Expectancy to Age (1):			82 years
9	Daughter, Natalie		8/7/2009	5.15
10	Normal Life Expectancy to Age (1):			80 years
11	With Three Person Household:			2014 Dollars
12	Average weekly earnings as welder:			$825
13	Annualized wage, 2014 $s:			$42,900
14	Plus Fringe Benefits as stated 12% of wage:			$5,148
15	Less Federal Income tax as stated 5% of wage:			-$2,145
16	Less Decedent's personal consumption 3 person family (28%)			-$12,012
17	Less potential savings at 5% of wage:			-$2,145
18	Net Balance Available for family financial support:			$31,746
19	With Two Person Household:			2027 Dollars
20	Annualized wage, 2027 $s:			$59,138
21	Plus Fringe Benefits as stated 12% of wage:			$7,097
22	Less Federal Income tax as stated 5% of AGI:			-$2,957
23	Less Decedent's personal consumption 2 person family (40%)			-$23,655
24	Less potential savings at 5% of wage:			-$2,957
25	Net Balance Available for family financial support:			$36,666
Economic Factors, Generally Applicable:				
1	Inflation (CPI) forecast (4,7):			2.0%
2	Real wage growth rate forecast (4,5,6):			0.5%
3	Nominal wage growth rate forecast:			2.5%
4	Nominal discount rate, tax free (3):			3.3%
5	Income Tax Rate applied (9):			5.0%
6	Benefits rate applied			12.0%
7	Decedent's Personal Consumption 3 person family (15):			28.0%
8	Decedent's Personal Consumption 2 person family (15):			40.0%
9	Average savings rate as % wage (16):			5.0%
Summary of Damage Calculations:				
1		Value Lost		Present Value
2	Lost Past Financial Support	$29,974		$29,974
3	Lost Future Financial Support	$2,201,192		$1,095,061
4	Total Lost Financial Support	$2,231,166		$1,125,034
5				
6	Lost Net Estate Accumulations	$278,609		$48,259
7				
8	TOTAL CALCULATED LOSSES:	$2,509,775		$1,173,293
5				

(1) Numbers in parenthesis indicates Referenced Source on attached list.

 printed on: 11/25/2014 14:18

PX 10

LOST FINANCIAL SUPPORT AND ESTATE ACCUMULATIONS
JOHNNY FITZGERALD

page 2

Economic Damages Worksheet

		age end of year			Projected	Savings	Cumulative Savings	Family Financial	Family Financial	Financial Support
	year	Decedent	Wife	Daughter	annual wage	Potential (5%)	Plus interest @ 3.3%/yr	Support Potential	Support Lost	cumulative loss
-1	2013	24	23	4	$8,330	$416	$416	$6,164	$6,164	$6,164
0	2014	25	24	5	$42,900	$2,145	$2,575	$31,746	$23,810	$29,974
							Loss to Sept. 30, 2014:			$29,974

		age end of year			Projected	Savings	Cumulative Savings	Family Financial	Present Value	Cumulative Present
	year	Decedent	Wife	Daughter	annual wage	Potential	Plus interest @ 3.3%/yr	Support Potential	Lost Financial Support	Value Lost Fin. Support
0	2014	25	24	5	$42,900	$2,145	$2,575	$7,937	$7,937	$7,937
1	2015	26	25	6	$43,973	$2,199	$4,859	$32,540	$31,500	$39,437
2	2016	27	26	7	$45,072	$2,254	$7,273	$33,353	$31,256	$70,693
3	2017	28	27	8	$46,199	$2,310	$9,823	$34,187	$31,014	$101,707
4	2018	29	28	9	$47,354	$2,368	$12,515	$35,042	$30,774	$132,481
5	2019	30	29	10	$48,537	$2,427	$15,354	$35,918	$30,536	$163,017
6	2020	31	30	11	$49,751	$2,488	$18,349	$36,816	$30,299	$193,316
7	2021	32	31	12	$50,995	$2,550	$21,504	$37,736	$30,064	$223,380
8	2022	33	32	13	$52,269	$2,613	$24,827	$38,679	$29,832	$253,212
9	2023	34	33	14	$53,576	$2,679	$28,325	$39,646	$29,601	$282,812
10	2024	35	34	15	$54,916	$2,746	$32,006	$40,638	$29,371	$312,184
11	2025	36	35	16	$56,289	$2,814	$35,876	$41,654	$29,144	$341,328
12	2026	37	36	17	$57,696	$2,885	$39,945	$42,695	$28,918	$370,246
13	2027	38	37	18	$59,138	$2,957	$44,220	$43,762	$28,694	$398,940
14	2028	39	38	19	$60,617	$3,031	$48,710	$44,856	$28,472	$427,412
15	2029	40	39	20	$62,132	$3,107	$53,424	$45,978	$28,252	$455,664
16	2030	41	40	21	$63,685	$3,184	$58,371	$47,127	$28,033	$483,697
17	2031	42	41	22	$65,277	$3,264	$63,561	$48,305	$27,816	$511,512
18	2032	43	42	23	$66,909	$3,345	$69,004	$49,513	$27,600	$539,112
19	2033	44	43	24	$68,582	$3,429	$74,711	$50,751	$27,386	$566,499
20	2034	45	44	25	$70,297	$3,515	$80,691	$52,020	$27,174	$593,673
21	2035	46	45	26	$72,054	$3,603	$86,957	$53,320	$26,964	$620,637
22	2036	47	46	27	$73,855	$3,693	$93,519	$54,653	$26,755	$647,392
23	2037	48	47	28	$75,702	$3,785	$100,390	$56,019	$26,548	$673,940
24	2038	49	48	29	$77,594	$3,880	$107,583	$57,420	$26,342	$700,283
25	2039	50	49	30	$79,534	$3,977	$115,110	$58,855	$26,138	$726,421
26	2040	51	50	31	$81,523	$4,076	$122,984	$60,327	$25,936	$752,357
27	2041	52	51	32	$83,561	$4,178	$131,221	$61,835	$25,735	$778,092
28	2042	53	52	33	$85,650	$4,282	$139,834	$63,381	$25,536	$803,628
29	2043	54	53	34	$87,791	$4,390	$148,838	$64,965	$25,338	$828,966
30	2044	55	54	35	$89,986	$4,499	$158,249	$66,589	$25,142	$854,107
31	2045	56	55	36	$92,235	$4,612	$168,083	$68,254	$24,947	$879,054
32	2046	57	56	37	$94,541	$4,727	$178,356	$69,960	$24,754	$903,808
33	2047	58	57	38	$96,905	$4,845	$189,087	$71,709	$24,562	$928,370
34	2048	59	58	39	$99,327	$4,966	$200,294	$73,502	$24,372	$952,742
35	2049	60	59	40	$101,811	$5,091	$211,994	$75,340	$24,183	$976,925
36	2050	61	60	41	$104,356	$5,218	$224,207	$77,223	$23,996	$1,000,921
37	2051	62	61	42	$106,965	$5,348	$236,954	$79,154	$23,810	$1,024,731
38	2052	63	62	43	$109,639	$5,482	$250,256	$81,133	$23,626	$1,048,357
39	2053	64	63	44	$112,380	$5,619	$264,133	$83,161	$23,443	$1,071,800
40	2054	65	64	45	$115,189	$5,759	$278,609	$85,240	$23,261	$1,095,061
41	2068	79	71	53	Future Lost Estate Value:		$278,609	Future Value Lost Financial Support:		$2,201,192
					Present Value of Lost Future Estate:		$48,259	Present Value Lost Financial Support:		$1,095,061

PX 10

SERVICES LOST TO HOUSEHOLD OF
JOHNNY FITZGERALD

page 1

Economic Factors Re: JOHNNY FITZGERALD

Date of analysis, years since d/d:	9/30/2014		0.94
Date of birth, current age would be:	10/24/89		24.93
Date of death (d/d) at age:	10/20/13		23.99
Normal Life Expectancy to Age (1):			79 years
Household Members:		Born	current age
Wife, Debra Fitzgerald		4/6/1990	24.48
Normal Life Expectancy to Age (1):			82 years
Daughter, Natalie		8/7/2009	5.15
Normal Life Expectancy to Age (1):			80 years
Services Lost:			annulized
Active Services, per family testimony, 14 hours/week, value @ $13/hr			$9,464
Passive Services provided 94 hours/week; value at $13/hr:			$63,544
Total Annual Value, Lost Services			$73,008

Note: Passive service can include security, protection and stand-by for active care. Passive services are rendered during time spent with family members, and are measured here net of those hours of active services already accounted for above and after the 60 hours normally devoted to employment, commuting and other hours away from home.

Economic Factors, Generally Applicable:

Inflation (CPI) forecast (4,7):	2.0%
Real wage growth rate forecast (4,5,6):	0.5%
Nominal wage growth rate forecast:	2.5%
Nominal discount rate, tax free (3):	3.3%

Summary of Damage Calculations:

	Value Lost	Present Value
Lost Past Active Services	$9,078	$9,078
Lost Future Active Services	$1,108,205	$426,446
Total Lost Active Services	$1,117,283	$435,524
Lost Past Passive Services	$60,949	$60,949
Lost Future Passive Services	$7,440,808	$2,863,283
Total Lost Protective Services	$7,501,757	$2,924,233
Total Lost Past Services	$70,027	$70,027
Total Lost Future Services	$8,549,013	$3,289,730
Total Lost Services	$8,619,040	$3,359,757

(1) Numbers in parenthesis indicates Referenced Source on attached list.

 printed on: 11/25/2014 20:53

PX 10

SERVICES LOST TO HOUSEHOLD OF
JOHNNY FITZGERALD

page 2

Economic Damages Worksheet

		age end of year			Projected Lost	Projected Lost		
	year	Decedent	Wife	Daughter	Active Services	Passive Services		
-1	2013	24	23	4	$1,838	$12,338		
0	2014	25	24	5	$7,240	$48,611		
	Past Loss to 9/30/2014:				$9,078	$60,949		

		age end of year			Projected Lost	Projected Lost	Present Value Annual	Present Value Annual
	year	Decedent	Wife	Daughter	Active Services	Passive Services	Lost Active Services	Lost Passive Services
0	2014	25	24	5	$2,413	$16,204	$2,413	$16,204
1	2015	26	25	6	$9,895	$66,435	$9,579	$64,313
2	2016	27	26	7	$10,142	$68,096	$9,504	$63,815
3	2017	28	27	8	$10,396	$69,799	$9,431	$63,321
4	2018	29	28	9	$10,655	$71,544	$9,358	$62,830
5	2019	30	29	10	$10,922	$73,332	$9,285	$62,344
6	2020	31	30	11	$11,195	$75,165	$9,213	$61,861
7	2021	32	31	12	$11,475	$77,045	$9,142	$61,382
8	2022	33	32	13	$11,762	$78,971	$9,071	$60,906
9	2023	34	33	14	$12,056	$80,945	$9,001	$60,435
10	2024	35	34	15	$12,357	$82,969	$8,931	$59,967
11	2025	36	35	16	$12,666	$85,043	$8,862	$59,502
12	2026	37	36	17	$12,983	$87,169	$8,793	$59,041
13	2027	38	37	18	$13,307	$89,348	$8,725	$58,584
14	2028	39	38	19	$13,640	$91,582	$8,658	$58,131
15	2029	40	39	20	$13,981	$93,871	$8,591	$57,680
16	2030	41	40	21	$14,330	$96,218	$8,524	$57,234
17	2031	42	41	22	$14,689	$98,624	$8,458	$56,790
18	2032	43	42	23	$15,056	$101,089	$8,393	$56,351
19	2033	44	43	24	$15,432	$103,616	$8,328	$55,914
20	2034	45	44	25	$15,818	$106,207	$8,263	$55,481
21	2035	46	45	26	$16,213	$108,862	$8,199	$55,051
22	2036	47	46	27	$16,619	$111,583	$8,136	$54,625
23	2037	48	47	28	$17,034	$114,373	$8,073	$54,202
24	2038	49	48	29	$17,460	$117,232	$8,010	$53,782
25	2039	50	49	30	$17,897	$120,163	$7,948	$53,366
26	2040	51	50	31	$18,344	$123,167	$7,887	$52,953
27	2041	52	51	32	$18,803	$126,246	$7,825	$52,542
28	2042	53	52	33	$19,273	$129,403	$7,765	$52,136
29	2043	54	53	34	$19,755	$132,638	$7,705	$51,732
30	2044	55	54	35	$20,248	$135,954	$7,645	$51,331
31	2045	56	55	36	$20,755	$139,352	$7,586	$50,934
32	2046	57	56	37	$21,273	$142,836	$7,527	$50,539

PX 10

SERVICES LOST TO HOUSEHOLD OF JOHNNY FITZGERALD									page 3
		age end of year			Projected Lost	Projected Lost	Present Value Annual	Present Value Annual	
	year	Decedent	Wife	Daughter	Active Services	Passive Services	Lost Active Services	Lost Passive Services	
33	2047	58	57	38	$21,805	$146,407	$7,469	$50,148	
34	2048	59	58	39	$22,350	$150,067	$7,411	$49,759	
35	2049	60	59	40	$22,909	$153,819	$7,354	$49,374	
36	2050	61	60	41	$23,482	$157,664	$7,297	$48,992	
37	2051	62	61	42	$24,069	$161,606	$7,240	$48,612	
38	2052	63	62	43	$24,671	$165,646	$7,184	$48,236	
39	2053	64	63	44	$25,287	$169,787	$7,128	$47,862	
40	2054	65	64	45	$25,920	$174,032	$7,073	$47,492	
41	2055	66	65	46	$26,568	$178,383	$7,018	$47,124	
42	2056	67	66	47	$27,232	$182,842	$6,964	$46,759	
43	2057	68	67	48	$27,913	$187,414	$6,910	$46,397	
44	2058	69	68	49	$28,610	$192,099	$6,857	$46,037	
45	2059	70	69	50	$29,326	$196,901	$6,804	$45,681	
46	2060	71	70	51	$30,059	$201,824	$6,751	$45,327	
47	2061	72	71	52	$30,810	$206,869	$6,699	$44,976	
48	2062	73	72	53	$31,581	$212,041	$6,647	$44,628	
49	2063	74	73	54	$32,370	$217,342	$6,595	$44,282	
50	2064	75	74	55	$33,179	$222,776	$6,544	$43,939	
51	2065	76	75	56	$34,009	$228,345	$6,493	$43,599	
52	2066	77	76	57	$34,859	$234,054	$6,443	$43,261	
53	2067	78	77	58	$35,731	$239,905	$6,393	$42,926	
54	2068	79	78	59	$36,624	$245,903	$6,344	$42,594	
					$1,108,205	$7,440,808	$426,446	$2,863,283	
					FV Active	FV Passive Serv.	PV Active	PV Passive Serv.	

PX 10

Referenced Sources: Economic Data

2009 Life Tables. Available at http://www.cdc.gov/nchs/data/nvsr/nvsr62/nvsr62_07.pdf

ATUS American Time Use Study, 2013 Results. Available at http://www.bls.gov/news.release/pdf/atus.pdf

Average Income Tax Rates by Income Categories, 2001–2012. Available at http://www.irs.gov/uac/SOI-Tax-Stats---Individual-Statistical-Tables-by-Size-of-Adjusted-Gross-Income

Consumer Expenditure Survey, Bureau of Labor Statistics. Available at http://www.bls.gov/cex/2013/aggregate/cusize.pdf and http://www.bls.gov/cex/

CPI-U May 2014 News Release – data by detailed expenditure categories. Available at http://www.bls.gov/news.release/pdf/cpi.pdf

Economic News Release, Compensation percent changes, Bureau of Labor Statistics. Available at http://www.bls.gov/news.release/eci.t04.htm

Employment Cost Index 2001–2014, Bureau of Labor Statistics. Available at http://www.bls.gov/web/eci/echistrynaics.pdf

Federal Reserve Bank Philadelphia, Survey of Economic Projections. Available at http://www.philadelphiafed.org/research-and-data/real-time-center/livingston-survey

Money Earnings by Age, Race, Education 2013, US Census Bureau, CPS. Available at http://www.census.gov/hhes/www/cpstables/032014/perinc/toc.htm

Medical Care Cost Projections, 2014–2022, Office of the Actuary, CMS. Unpublished 2014.

Michael R. Ruble, Robert T. Patton, and David M. Nelson, *Patton-Nelson Personal Consumption Tables 2005–06*, JOURNAL OF FORENSIC ECONOMICS, Vol. 20 No.3, 217–225.

Labor Force Participation Rates to 2018. Bureau of Labor Statistics, U.S. Dep't of Labor. Available at http://www.bls.gov/opub/mlr/2009/11/art3full.pdf

Labor Force Participation Rates to 2022. Bureau of Labor Statistics, U.S. Dep't of Labor. Available at http://www.bls.gov/opub/mlr/2013/article/labor-force-projections-to-2022-the-labor-force-participation-rate-continues-to-fall.htm

Labor Force Participation Rates to 2050. Bureau of Labor Statistics, U.S. Dep't of Labor. Available at http://www.bls.gov/opub/mlr/2002/05/art2full.pdf

U.S. Historical Interest Rates, Nominal and Real, U.S. Treasury. Available at http://www.treasury.gov/resource-center/data-chart-center/interest-rates/Pages/Historic-LongTerm-Rate-Data-Visualization.aspx

U.S. Treasury and Municipal Bond Yields. Available at http://www.bloomberg.com/markets/rates-bonds/government-bonds/us/

PX 11

**Screenshot of Text Message
from Johnny Fitzgerald to Debra Fitzgerald**

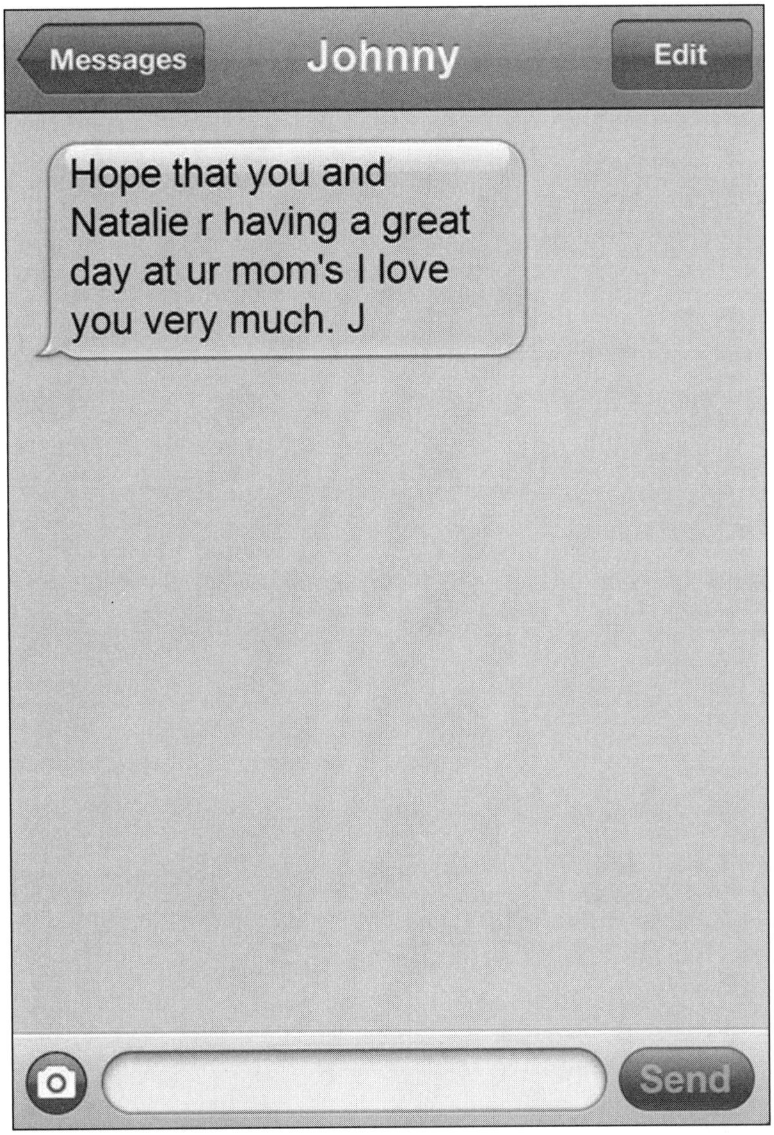

PX 12

Photo of Debra and Johnny Fitzgerald

DX 26

Railroad Accident Report

WIRE REPORT F-27
CONDUCTOR AND/OR MAINTENANCE MACHINE OPERATORS

ON—TRACK EQUIPMENT ACCIDENT/INCIDENT REPORT
—IMMEDIATE NOTIFICATION—

ALL "FAILED JOURNALS" AND "BROKEN WHEELS" OCCURRING ON MAIN OR BRANCH TRACKS MUST BE REPORTED.

(Complete all appropriate sections of this report and send to Superintendent and to Region Vice President by quickest means of communication)

To: Superintendent Date: 10/26/13 From: M. Edwards Division: Investigation

Types or types of on-track equipment involvement (Check all appropriate boxes)

- ☐ Derailment - —Complete pages 1 and 2
- ☐ Collision between on-track equipment consists —Complete pages 1, 2, and 3
- ☒ Rail-highway grade crossing collision —Complete pages 1, 2, and 4
- ☐ Obstruction incident —Complete pages 1 and 2
- ☐ Fire damage to locomotives, cars or contents —Complete pages 1, 2, and 5
- ☐ Hazardous material incident —Complete pages 1 and 2
  Form 15957 for each car of hazardous material derailed or damaged
- ☐ Casualty to person(s) —Complete pages 1 and 2
  Form 15016 for each casualty

(Hot boxes, broken knuckles, sticking brakes, etc., which do not result in any of the above, and require repairs only to that part involved, need not be reported on F-27 On-Track Equipment Accident/Incident Report.)

F-27 INIT.	F-27 NUMBER	ACCIDENT DATE YEAR MONTH DAY	TIME HOUR MIN	SUB-DIVN	STATE CODE	MAIN TRACK BLOCKED? (Y or N) Y
		13 10 20	17 47		NT	CLEARED BY TIME 1900 DATE 10/20/13

ROAD LINE SGMT.	MILEPOST LOCATION (100ths)	TRACK OWNER	NEAREST STATION NO.	NAME OF NEAREST STATION
	.	N&W	047	WELLINGTON

TYPE OF INCIDENT: 12

01 DERAILMENT; 02 HEAD-ON COLLISION; 03 READ—END COLLISION; 04 SIDE COLLISION; 05 RAKING COLLISION; 06 BROKEN TRAIN COLL; 07 HGX COLLISION; 08 RR CROSSING COLL; 09 OBSTRUCTION INCIDENT; 10 EXPLOSION-DENOTATION; 11 FIRE-VIOLENT RUPTURE; 12 OTHER R - H

TEMP. (Degrees)	VISIBILITY (1—DAWN 2—DAY 3—DUSK 4—DARK)	WEATHER (1—CLEAR 2—CLOUDY 3—RAIN 4—FOG 5—SLEET 6—SNOW)
58	2	1

METHOD(S) OF OPERATION = PRIMARY - SECONDARY - ADDITIONAL: B

A—NON-ABS; B—INTERLOCKING; C—CAB SIGNAL; D—ABS; E—CTC; F—AUTO. TRAIN STOP; G—YARD RULES; H—TIMETABLE; I—RADIO; K—VERBAL PERMISSION; L—TRAIN ORDERS (INCL. TWC); M—OTHER; N—YARD LIMITS (ON MAIN TRACK WITHIN YARD LIMITS)

ACCIDENT AT TURNOUT? (1-YES 2-NO)	ACCIDENT IN CURVE (1-YES 2-NO)	TRACK NAME OR NUMBER	TYPE OF TRACK (1-MAIN 2-YARD 3-SIDING 4-INDUSTRY)
2	2	SINGLE MAIN	1

FRA TRACK CLASS (X-EXCEPTED 1-CLASS 1 2-CLASS 2 3-CLASS 3 4-CLASS 4 5-CLASS 5 6-CLASS 6)	COUNTY OR PROVIDENCE IN WHICH ACCIDENT OCCURED
4	DOUGLAS

PRIMARY CAUSE	CONTRIB. CAUSE	LOCOMOTIVE CAUSED? L-YES	BROKEN RAIL WT.	YEAR RAIL LAID	EXAMPLE: EXPRESS 1958 AS 958

SYSTEM OR FOREIGN RESPONSIBILITY (S-SYSTEM F-FOREIGN)	TERMINAL? ENTER "T" IF: DENVER, KANSAS CITY, OR, TWIN CITIES	REPORTABLE TO FRA? R-REP	FOREIGN CARRIER ACCIDENT REPORT NUMBER
S			

NAME OF INDUSTRY IF TRACK OWNER IS "XX" (INDUSTRY)

DESCRIPTION OF ACCIDENT:
Auto ran into freight train XT471 (4 engines, 85 cars) at cars 1/2
Crossing # 74647C, County Road, Wellington

CASUALTIES TO PERSONS—LIST AND COMPLETE FORM 15016 FOR EACH CASUALTY INVOLVED

FI	MI	LAST NAME	STREET ADDRESS	CITY OR TOWN	STATE
J		Fitzgerald	16 Meadowbrook Lane	Wellington	NT

SIGNATURE: [signature] TITLE: Investigator DATE: 10/26/13

FORM 15012 9-84 Printed In U. S. A.

DX 26

Railroad Accident Report

PAGE 2: INFORMATION FOR CONSIST NO. 1 INVOLVED IN ACCIDENT

CONSIST OWNER: N & W
TYPE OF EQUIPMENT: A
A—FREIGHT TRAIN, B—PSGR. TRAIN, C—MIXED TRAIN, E—SINGLE CAR, F—MOTOR CAR, G—HI-RAIL CAR, H—PUSH CAR, I—ON TRACK MAINT. MACHINE, J—CUT OF CARS, K—SWITCH ENGINE, L—SW. ENG. WITH CARS, M—LITE UNITS

SPEED OF CONSIST: 48
SPEED EST. OR RECORDED: E (E-EST. R-REC.)
POSITION OF CONSIST: 1 (1-TRAIN (UNITS PULLING), 2-TRAIN (UNITS PUSHING), 3-TRAIN (STANDING), 4-CAR(S) (MOVING), 5-CAR(S) STANDING, 6-LIGHT LOCOS (MOVING), 7-LIGHT LOCOS (STANDING), 8-OTHER)

TIMETABLE DIRECTION: 1 (1-NORTH, 2-SOUTH, 3-EAST, 4-WEST)
HEADLIGHT: 1 (1-ON, 2-OFF, 3-N/A) (HGX ONLY)
AMBER/STROBE (HGX ONLY): 3 (1-ON, 2-OFF, 3-NOT EQUIPPED)
REFLECTORIZED (HGX ONLY) MARKINGS = 1 (1-YES, 2-NO, 3-UNKNOWN)

WHISTLE SOUNDED?: 1 (1-YES, 2-NO, 3-NOT EQUIPPED)
BELL RINGING?: 1 (1-YES, 2-NO, 3-NOT EQUIPPED)
CONSIST IDENTIFICATION NUMBER: 15163

TOTAL EQUIPMENT DAMAGE E/A THIS CONSIST:
TOTAL 'FRA' TRACK DAMAGE E/A THIS CONSIST:
DAMAGE TO LOCOMOTIVES ON E/A THIS CONSIST:

DAMAGE TO CARS ON E/A THIS CONSIST:
DAMAGE TO NON-RAILROAD E/A PROPERTY:
DAMAGE TO BRIDGES E/A:

DAMAGE TO SIGNALS DUE TO E/A THIS CONSIST:
DAMAGE TO COMMUNICATIONS E/A DUE TO THIS CONSIST:
DAMAGE TO RAILROAD E/A STRUCTURES:

NUMBER FATALITIES ON THIS CONSIST: 0
NUMBER INJURED ON THIS CONSIST (REP FRA): 0
WAS THIS CONSIST UNATTENDED AT TIME OF THE ACCIDENT?: 2 (1-YES, 2-NO)

INFORMATION FOR HAZARDOUS MATERIAL CARS IN THIS CONSIST	NO. CARS CARRYING	NO. CARS DAMAGED ON DERAILED	NO. CARS RELEASING HAZARDOUS MATERIAL	NUMBER OF PERSONS EVACUATED

	INITIAL	NUMBER	POSITION	LOADED OR EMPTY? (L—LOAD, E—EMPTY)
FIRST CAR OR LOCOMOTIVE OF THIS CONSIST INVOLVED IN THE ACCIDENT				
CAR OR LOCOMOTIVE UNIT IN THIS CONSIST CAUSING THE ACCIDENT (MECHANICAL ONLY)				

	HEAD END	MID—MANUAL	MID—REMOTE	REAR-END MANUAL	REAR-END REMOTE
NUMBER OF LOCOMOTIVE UNITS IN THIS CONSIST	4				
NUMBER OF LOCOMOTIVE UNITS IN THIS CONSIST DERAILED					

NOTE: IF OWNERSHIP OF LOCOMOTIVE UNITS IS OTHER THAN BN, INDICATE OWNER-

	NUMBER	NUMBER	NUMBER	NUMBER	NUMBER	NUMBER
LOCOMOTIVE IDENTIFICATION NO.s IN THIS CONSIST (FROM HEAD-END, 1st THRU 6TH:						
LOCOMOTIVE IDENTIFICATION NUMBERS IN THIS CONSIST (7th Through 12th If Appropriate):						

	LOADED FREIGHT	PSGR LOADED	EMPTY FREIGHT	PSGR EMPTY	CAB
NUMBER OF CARS IN THIS CONSIST	21		64		
NUMBER OF CARS DERAILED IN CONSIST	1				

RAILROAD ACCOUNT CARS IN:
TYPE OF SERVICE (FRT TRAINS, CUTS OF CARS, LOCO CONSISTS): R
C-UNIT COAL, G-UNIT GRAIN, O-UNIT ORE, R-REGULAR FREIGHT, T-UNIT TACONITE

TRAILING TONS	NUMBER OF CREW MEMBERS ON THIS CONSIST	ENGINEERS	FIREPERSONS	CONDUCTORS	BRAKEPERSONS
4033		1	2	1	1

	HRS	MIN		FI	MI	LAST NAME
ENGINEER—ON DUTY	4	20	NAME OF ENGINEER ON THIS CONSIST	S		SMOLEN
CONDUCTOR—ON DUTY	4	20	NAME OF CONDUCTOR ON THIS CONSIST	R		APRIL

DX 26

Railroad Accident Report

PAGE 4: COMPLETE THIS PAGE FOR ALL RAIL-HIGHWAY GRADE CROSSING ACCIDENTS

OCCURANCE CODE: 6 0 5
601—PEDESTRIAN SRUCK BY TRAIN
602—MOTOR VEHICLE STRUCK BY TRAIN
603—OTHER VEHICLE, MACHINE, OR ANIMAL STRUCK BY TRAIN
604-PEDESTRIAN RAN INTO TRAIN OR PASSED OVER-THRU-UNDER CARS
605-MOTOR VEHICLE RAN INTO TRAIN
609-OTHER ACCIDENT AT RAIL-HWY GRADE CROSSING SITE

TYPE OF HIGHWAY USER: A
A-AUTO, B-TRUCK, C-TRUCK-TRAILER, D-BUS, E-SCHOOL BUS, F-MOTORCYCLE, G-PEDESTRIAN, H-BICYCLE, I-FARM VEHICLE, J-GASOLINE TRANSPORT, K-OTHER

DIRECTION OF HIGHWAY USER: 3 (1-NORTH, 2-SOUTH, 3-EAST, 4-WEST)
SPEED OF HWY USER: 5 0 Est.
POSITION OF HIGHWAY USER: 3 (1-STALLED ON CROSSING, 2-STOPPED ON CROSSING, 3-MOVING OVER CROSSING)

MOTORIST ACTION: 3 (1-DROVE AROUND OR THRU GATES, 2-STOPPED AND THEN PROCEEDED, 3-DID NOT STOP, 4-OTHER, 5-UNKNOWN)
SECOND TRAIN INVOLVED? (MOTORIST STRUCK BY SECOND TRAIN AT XING): 2 (1-YES 2-NO 3-UNKNOWN)

MOTORIST PASSED STANDING VEHICLE?: 2 (1-YES 2-NO 3-UNKNOWN)
DRIVER IN VEHICLE?: 1 (1-YES 2-NO (BLANK IF UNKNOWN))

DRIVER CONDITION: 1 (BLANK IF UNKNOWN) (1-FATALLY INJURED, 2-INJURED (REP-FRA), 3-UNINJURED (NON-REP))
NO. OCCUPANTS FATAL (INCLUDING DRIVER): 1
NO. OCCUPANTS INJURED (REP FRA) (INCLUDING DRIVER):

TOTAL NUMBER OF OCCUPANTS: 1 (INCLUDE DRIVER)
EST. DAMAGE TO HIGHWAY USER: 5 0 0 0
HAZARDOUS MATERIALS: 4 (1-HWY USER TRANSPORTING, 2-RAIL CONSIST TRANSPORTING, 3-BOTH TRANSPORTING, 4-NEITHER TRANSPORTING)

DOT-AAR IDENTIFICATION NO.:
ROAD CONDITION: 1 (1-DRY, 2-WET, 3-ICY, 4-SNOW PACKED)
ROAD SURFACE TYPE: 3 (1-ASPHALT, 2-CONCRETE, 3-GRAVEL, 4-DIRT)

HIGHEST LEVEL OF CROSSING PROTECTION: 0 7
01-GATES, 02-CANTILEVER FLSHG LIGHTS, 03-STANDARD FLSHG LIGHTS, 04-WIG WAGS, 05-HIGHWAY TRAFFIC SIGNALS, 06-AUDIBLE WARNING, 07-CROSSBUCKS ONLY, 08-STOP SIGNS, 09-WATCHMAN, 10-FLAGGED BY CREW, 11-OTHER, 12-NONE

LOCATION OF PROTECTION: 3 (BLANK IF NONE) (1-BOTH SIDES OF CROSSING, 2-SIDE OF VEHICLE APPROACH, 3-OPPOSITE SIDE OF VEHICLE APPROACH)
HWY TRAFFIC SIGNALS INTERCONNECTED?: 2 (1-CONNECTED WITHIN 500 FEET, 2-NOT CONNECTED WITHIN 500 FT, 3-NOT KNOWN)

PROTECTION OPERATING?: 1 (1-YES, 2-NO, (BLANK))
VIEW RESTRICTED?: 4,5 (1-PERMANENT STRUCTURE, 2-STANDING RR EQUIPMENT, 3-PASSING TRAIN, 4-TOPOGRAPHY, 5-VEGETATION, 6-HIGHWAY VEHICLE, 7-OTHER, 8-NOT OBSTRUCTED)

CROSSING ILLUMINATED?: 2 (1-YES, 2-NO)
CROSSING NAME OR NUMBER: 7 4 6 4 7 C C O U N T Y R O A D

TYPE OF CROSSING?: C (A-PRIVATE, B-CITY, C-COUNTY, D-STATE, E-U.S.)
ADVANCE WARNING?: 2 (1-YES, 2-NO)
REPORTABLE BY BN TO FRA?: (R-REP., N-NON-REP)
REP RAIL ACCT ALSO?: (1-YES, 2-NO)

YEAR OF VEH: 2 0 0 2
MAKE OF VEHICLE: F O R D
MODEL OF VEHICLE: S E D A N 4 D R

OWNER OF VEHICLE	FI	MI	LAST NAME	STREET ADDRESS	CITY	STATE
	J		F I T Z G E R A L D	1 6 M E A D O W B R	W E L L I N G T N	N T

DISPOSITION OF VEHICLE & EST. DAMAGE:
Transported by wrecker Totaled

NAME OF DRIVER OR PEDESTRIAN	FI	MI	LAST NAME	STREET ADDRESS	CITY	STATE
	J		Fitzgerald	16 Meadowbrook Lane	Wellington	N T

☐ INJURED ☐ FATAL ☐ NOT INJURED (X)

NAME OF OCCUPANT	FI	MI	LAST NAME	STREET ADDRESS	CITY	STATE

☐ INJURED ☐ FATAL ☐ NOT INJURED (X)

NAME OF OCCUPANT	FI	MI	LAST NAME	STREET ADDRESS	CITY	STATE

☐ INJURED ☐ FATAL ☐ NOT INJURED (X)

DISPOSITION OF INJURED OR FATAL OCCUPANTS
Removed by Erickson's Mortuary

DX 27

Written Statement of Matt Green

NITA & WESTERN RAILWAY COMPANY
STATEMENT OF TRAIN AND ENGINE CREWS

This form is to be used by all members of train and engine crews in rendering statements concerning accidents in which train or engines are involved with vehicles or outsiders. The statement must be completed by all crew members and promptly mailed or delivered to the division superintendent.

Place of accident Wellington Division Main

Date of accident Oct 20 2013 Time 5:47 pm

Train no. XT 471 Speed of train 48 Direction N Weather calm

Was horn sounded? yes Bell ringing? yes

Was stationary headlight burning? yes Bright? yes Dim?

Was oscillating headlight operating? Bright? Dim?

Damage to railway equipment Boxcar & tracks operable

Make of vehicle Ford Year 02 License no.

Direction of vehicle East Speed 50 MPH

Driver Age Address

Owner Address

Other occupants, ages, addresses

Damage to vehicle Wiped out

Were there any injuries? Yes No

Type of crossing protection Crossbucks Operating? Yes ✓ No

Condition of crossing good

Where were you at time of accident? Engine #2

Describe accident (include type and place of brake application, when vehicle, trespasser, pedestrian, or injured person first see, etc.)

Didn't see it - engine went into emergency
Driver dead at scene

Names and addresses of outside witnesses Neighbor - didn't get his name he spoke to the trooper

Did police investigate accident? Yes ✓ No State County City

Signature Matt Green

Address 716 Main Nita City, NT

Date Oct 20, 2013 Occupation Breakman Age 42

DX 28

Written Statement of Steve Smolen

NITA & WESTERN RAILWAY COMPANY
STATEMENT OF TRAIN AND ENGINE CREWS

This form is to be used by all members of train and engine crews in rendering statements concerning accidents in which train or engines are involved with vehicles or outsiders. The statement must be completed by all crew members and promptly mailed or delivered to the division superintendent.

Place of accident Wellington Division Main

Date of accident 10/20/13 Time 5:47 pm

Train no. XT471 Speed of train 45-50 Direction North Weather Clear

Was horn sounded? yes Bell ringing? yes

Was stationary headlight burning? yes Bright? ✓ Dim? ____

Was oscillating headlight operating? ____ Bright? ____ Dim? ____

Damage to railway equipment Boxcar: Trucks & side tracks operable

Make of vehicle 02 Ford Year 02 License no. NT DGF-459

Direction of vehicle East Speed 50 MPH

Driver Johnny Fitzgerald Age 25 Address 16 Meadowbrooke Lane

Owner Same Address Wellington

Other occupants, ages, addresses None

Damage to vehicle total

Were there any injuries? Yes ✓ No ____

Type of crossing protection crossbucks Operating? Yes ____ No ____

Condition of crossing good

Where were you at time of accident? First Engine

Describe accident (include type and place of brake application, when vehicle, trespasser, pedestrian, or injured person first see, etc.) car hit boxcar train into emergency

Names and addresses of outside witnesses ____

Did police investigate accident? Yes ✓ No ____ State ____ County ____ City ____

Signature Steve Smolen

Address 449 Clearmeadow Dr Nita City, NT

Date 10/20, 20 13 Occupation Engineer Age 38

DX 29

Supplement to Incident Report, October 26, 2013

Re: Train XT471 From: Mark Edwards

Crossing #74647C Investigator, Nita & Western Railroad

Rail-Highway

On October 20, 2013, at approximately 6:00 p.m., I was called to go to the subject crossing to investigate an incident. I arrived at approximately 6:20 p.m., briefly interviewed the train personnel, and instructed the engineer and brakeman to write out their statements. I spoke with the state trooper (Mike Benjamin #122) and reported to him that the train was traveling at approximately 48 mph per the engineer, confirmed by speed tape. I examined the train and the car wreckage, instructed the train crew to re-rail the train, and supervised the removal of the car from the tracks. I then examined the crossing, discovered two gouge marks near the tracks where the car had run into the train, and also observed the condition of the crossing sign. Because it was after sunset, I felt that I could not take adequate pictures of the scene that day. The trooper had taken some pictures that I felt would be useful.

I returned two days later, October 22, at 2:30 p.m., to take photographs of the scene. Photos 7, 8, 9, 10, and 11 were taken at eye level from a distance 50 feet west of the crossing. These pictures were taken in order to develop a panorama view of the crossing and tracks and to simulate what the driver would have seen at that distance. Photos 12, 13, and 14 were taken in the same fashion and with the same purpose at a distance of 75 feet west. Photos 15, 16, and 17 were also taken in the same manner and with the same purpose at a distance of 100 feet west. Photos 20 and 21 were taken from a point 200 feet west of the crossing in the same manner and with the same purpose; the tracks are clearly visible as is the crossing sign. The crossing sign was in adequate condition for its use but required some repair, which I authorized. It was located at the north side of the tracks and had weathered lettering on both sides. I filed report 376 (Request for Equipment Installation) on October 22. Coupled with the request was a suggestion to place a crossing sign on the south side of the road, facing west. I also examined the road to the west and found no advance warning sign on the road. I requested placement of a sign by the sign department on October 22 using another report 376.

I examined the records of the railroad and found only one prior incident at this crossing, which occurred in 2000. Only minor property damage occurred when a farmer's pickup had been hit by a train at night after the truck had been stolen and left on the tracks.

On October 25, I contacted the brakeman to come to my office for a statement as to exactly what he saw. The brakeman submitted the statement.

DX 1

Edwards Photo 7 (10-22-13)

DX 2

Edwards Photo 8 (10-22-13)

DX 3

Edwards Photo 9 (10-22-13)

DX 4

Edwards Photo 10 (10-22-13)

DX 5

Edwards Photo 11 (10-22-13)

DX 6

Edwards Photo 7–11 (10-22-13)

DX 7

Edwards Photo 12 (10-22-13)

DX 8

Edwards Photo 13 (10-22-13)

DX 9

Edwards Photo 14 (10-22-13)

DX 10

Edwards Photo 12–14 (10-22-13)

DX 11

Edwards Photo 15 (10-22-13)

DX 12

Edwards Photo 16 (10-22-13)

DX 13

Edwards Photo 17 (10-22-13)

DX 14

Edwards Photo 15–17 (10-22-13)

DX 15

Edwards Photo 20 (10-22-13)

DX 16

Edwards Photo 21 (10-22-13)

Statement of Matt Green

My name is Matt Green, age forty-two, married, and I live at 716 Main Street, Nita City. I am employed by the Nita & Western Railroad as a brakeman. I have been with the railroad for about fourteen years. Before that I was a truck driver for the United States Army, serving in Germany.

On October 20, 2013, I was working as a brakeman for the second engine (#1964) on Train XT471, which is the local freight train from Lisle to Nita City. The engineer was Steve Smolen, and the conductor in the first engine (#1563) was Rich April. Our train consisted of four engines, followed by eighty-five cars (twenty-one loaded, sixty-four empty) and had a total weight of 4,033 tons. As we moved north on the single line track, we were traveling at approximately forty-eight mph when we were hit by a car at crossing #74647C. I was seated in the second engine, left-hand side. As we approached the crossing, we passed the whistle board and the whistle began to blow. I was looking left at an angle toward the road, because my responsibility is to look for oncoming traffic. At about 1,200 feet away, I could see about 150 feet up the road, but could see more of the road as we got closer. At 350 feet from the crossing, growth and shrubbery on the road blocked my view of part of the road. There were weeds along the railroad right of way, but they did not block my view. Just before the crossing, I looked up the road and could see about 350 feet to the top of the hill, but could not see the road all of the way to the hilltop because the road dips. At no point did I see any cars coming.

It is also the brakeman's responsibility to look over the rear of the train when you have the opportunity. Because we were coming up on a curve, after the crossing I began to turn in my seat to look back at the train. I had my back to the side window at the time of the impact. I heard a sound like the shattering of glass and I looked out of the back window and saw rock and dirt flying. I only realized what had happened after the train had stopped. At the time of the collision, I looked at the speed tape recorder, and it was showing forty-eight mph.

After the train stopped, I went back along the train on the east side looking for whatever had caused the train to emergency. Rich April was on the west side. The first thing we saw was, of course, the remains of a car between the rails, after the first car, and before the rest of the train. Then we started walking along the rest of the train and saying, "Here's another part of the car," until Rich found Mr. Fitzgerald. The trooper was on the scene by this time, and I stayed to watch over the body until the mortuary arrived.

The weather was clear and dry, the gravel road was in good condition, and the crossing was protected by a crossbuck sign.

At the time of the accident, I was seated twelve feet above the ground in the second engine. The measurements of the four engines and the box car are:

Unit 1	(#1563)	55 feet, 11 inches
Unit 2	(#1964)	56 feet, 2 inches
Unit 3	(#1560)	55 feet, 11 inches
Unit 4	(#1965)	56 feet, 2 inches
Box Car	#1	44 feet, 4 inches

I have read this statement and it is correct to the best of my recollection and belief.

Matt Green

Matt Green

Signed at Nita City, Nita, on October 25, 2013

Mark Edwards

Witnessed: Mark Edwards

Investigator for Nita & Western Railroad

Memo from Railroad Investigator
to Colton & McLeod Law Firm

To: Colton & McLeod, Attorneys

From: Mark Edwards, Investigator, Nita & Western Railroad

Date: January 29, 2014

Subject: Incident of October 20, 2013

At your request and instruction, I went to the scene of the incident on January 28 at 11:00 a.m. to take additional photos of the scene and a simulated train.

Photos 1 through 8 were taken at a distance of 250 feet west of the crossing, looking east, and observing a freight train with four pulling engines. The crossing is clearly visible as is the train. As you can see, the crossing now contains two crossing signs. The four engines are of the same size and length as the train involved in this incident, as is the first box car.

Photo 9 was taken 75 feet east of the tracks, looking west.

I was also asked to provide some background on myself. I have been employed by Nita & Western for ten and a-half-years and have been serving as an investigator for the last eight years. I am thirty-nine years old and worked as claims adjuster for an insurance company between high school and my employment with Nita & Western.

DX 17

Edwards Photo 1 (1-28-14)

DX 18

Edwards Photo 2 (1-28-14)

DX 19

Edwards Photo 3 (1-28-14)

DX 20

Edwards Photo 4 (1-28-14)

DX 21

Edwards Photo 5 (1-28-14)

DX 22

Edwards Photo 6 (1-28-14)

DX 23

Edwards Photo 7 (1-28-14)

DX 24

Edwards Photo 8 (1-28-14)

DX 25

Edwards Photo 9 (1-28-14)

Deposition of Emily Field*

March 20, 2014

My name is Emily Field. I was born in Wellington, Nita, on July 2, 1990. I am married to Paul Field, and we live with our nine-month-old daughter, Cameron, at 234 Deerfield in Marion, approximately 250 miles from Wellington. Both Paul and I grew up in Wellington, and Paul is two years older than me. Paul is employed at Acme Insurance as a claims adjuster, and I am a stay-at-home mom.

Paul, Johnny Fitzgerald, and I were best friends, having grown up together and were classmates at school. In fact, Johnny was the best man at our wedding on July 4, 2012. Johnny and I dated in high school, but I was more serious about him than he was about me. He began to date Debi, and they got married real quick. I didn't get to see much of Johnny after that. I got to be friendly again with Johnny and met Debi when I started dating Paul about a year before our wedding, and we really got close during a camping trip that summer. As a matter of fact, Johnny and I had a long talk about my marrying Paul, because I was afraid that it would affect his relationship with Paul. I still felt a lot for Johnny. I even kidded that we ought to sneak away that night and be together one last time before I told Paul I would marry him. Johnny said that me marrying Paul would be the greatest thing that could happen to Paul. To not marry him would hurt Paul, and Johnny, very much.

After Paul and I got married and moved to Marion, we always tried to get together with the Fitzgeralds whenever we came to Wellington to visit Paul's mom and dad, Amy and Lonny. I had a better relationship with Johnny than with Debi. For some reason, Debi was sometimes cool toward me. I think that she may have been jealous that Paul, Johnny, and I had such a strong friendship and that we always kidded around so much. Maybe she thought I still had feelings for Johnny. Debi was a "city girl" from Nita City and really didn't think much of people from the country. We did get along pretty well though.

On October 19, 2013, we traveled to Wellington with our new baby to visit with my in-laws and to help celebrate the birthday of one of our friends, Greg Carlisle. Johnny and Debi were going to stay

* The transcript of Emily Field's deposition was excerpted so that only her answers are reprinted here. Assume that this is a true and accurate rendering of those answers.

over at the house that night. At about 5:30 p.m., the Fitzgeralds arrived, and Johnny went downstairs to play pool with Paul and Greg. Debi and her five-year-old daughter, Natalie, were with me, my mother-in-law, and my baby. I could tell that something was bothering Johnny and Debi because they seemed very quiet. The guys left about eight o'clock to go to Rocco's for dinner and beer. Debi and I started to prepare the children's dinner. I had to go to the store for some diapers, and I asked Debi if she wanted to go with me. We left in our car at about 8:45 to go to the store, which was about a mile away. We got the diapers pretty quickly and came back to the house. We fed the children and put them to sleep. At about 9:30 p.m., we left in the car to go to Rocco's to meet the guys.

We got to Rocco's shortly thereafter and stayed for about one hour, having two beers each. I danced with Johnny for one dance and asked him what he wanted for his birthday. He said something like "a new life," or something, and I asked him if there was anything wrong. He said that he wanted to talk, and we went to a corner booth for a few minutes. He said that he and Debi were having a tough time. She had met a guy at her job and she started spending a lot of time with him. She and Johnny had had an argument and she had packed clothes for herself and Natalie, and she and Natalie were going to leave Johnny the next day to go to live at her parents' home for a while until they straightened things out. He really wanted to talk to Paul, but felt he really couldn't bring up the situation. He said that he really couldn't live without Debi and Natalie, and that maybe he should drive his car into a bridge or something to end it all, but I felt that he really didn't mean it. Needless to say, I was very surprised that Johnny was telling me this. I said let's wait until everyone comes home tonight, and I will ask Paul to talk to Johnny before everyone leaves on Sunday. We then went back to our table.

At about 10:45, I called back to check on the baby. My mother-in-law told me the baby had just woken up, and I decided to go home to nurse the baby. Debi and I left, but we didn't talk about Johnny during the ride. We went back to the house, and I nursed the baby and fell asleep. Debi stayed in the TV room alone. Sometime later, I don't know exactly what time, Johnny helped Paul into our bedroom, because Paul had a little too much to drink. I was half asleep at the time and told Johnny we would see him in the morning and we could talk then.

The next morning, I woke up at about 5:00 a.m. and found that Johnny and Debi's car was gone and their bed had not been slept in. I then went back to sleep. When I woke up again around 8:30, I asked Paul how he felt and if Johnny had said anything last night about any problems at home. Paul said that Johnny seemed a little moody, but hadn't said anything specific. I said that maybe he should call Johnny that day to see if everything was okay. I didn't want to tell Paul about what Johnny had told me, thinking that it should come from Johnny. Paul said he would call that afternoon because he needed to talk to Johnny about the hunting trip they were going on the following week. Paul went back to sleep.

At about ten o'clock, Debi called my cell phone. Debi said she was calling to say goodbye and asked me to have Paul call Johnny before we left. I told her that Paul was going to call back later that day. She thanked us for being such good friends and hung up.

Paul tried to call Johnny at about one o'clock and then again at three o'clock, thinking that Johnny would be watching football games, but there was no answer. We tried again at 7:00 p.m., but again there was no answer on either his home or cell phone. I then called Debi's cell phone to tell her that we hadn't talked to Johnny yet. Debi said she didn't know where Johnny would be, but to keep trying, that maybe he had just gone out for a pizza. At about 11:30 p.m., we got a phone call from Debi's mother, Mrs. Kay. She told me that while Debi was doing laundry, they had gotten a phone call that Johnny had been killed in a train accident. Mrs. Kay had gone to tell her, and Debi had fainted. They had to take her to the hospital. When Debi woke up, she told Mrs. Kay to call Paul and me to let us know what had happened. I gave Paul the bad news and also told him about what Johnny had told me about their family problems and Debi's leaving Johnny. Paul said no wonder Johnny killed himself.

Although Paul didn't want me to talk to Debi again, I spoke with her at the funeral on Wednesday. She told me, "I don't know what I have done to deserve this, but whatever it was, it's too late now."

We didn't talk anymore because she started crying. Paul and I went back to Marion right after the funeral. Paul was really broken up. He had lost his best friend. He is still upset over the whole matter.

About a week after the funeral, my mother-in-law sent us a newspaper article written by Debi's mother. She wrote that Johnny's death was the railroad's fault. I guess she couldn't believe that Johnny would kill himself. Under the circumstances, I guess that Johnny took the only way he thought he had.

I have read this deposition, and the answers are correct to the best of my knowledge and belief.

Emily Field

Harold Bench

Emily Field

Harold Bench
Notary Public

March 20, 2014

Deposition of Paul Field*

April 28, 2014

My name is Paul Field. I was born in Wellington, Nita, on September 11, 1988. I am married to Emily Field, and we have one daughter, Cameron. We live in Marion, Nita. I have agreed to give you lawyers this deposition over the telephone, but I will not sign anything and will not willingly testify in this case. I will not help Debi Fitzgerald in this lawsuit after what she did to Johnny, but I feel bad for Natalie also. I will tell you this: the railroad is at fault also for not putting up automatic crossing gates at the crossing.

I knew Johnny Fitzgerald all my life. He was like a brother to me. We went through school together and spent most of our time together. He was the best friend a person could have. We always went hunting together every fall. In fact, we were planning to go hunting the week after he died. He was a great guy.

I know Debi Fitzgerald. She started to go out with Johnny in high school, although she was from Nita City. She and Johnny had met at a dance the summer of 2007. Johnny had been dating my Emily during the winter, but he broke up with her when he started to date Debi. Debi got pregnant, and they got married. I wasn't able to be at the wedding because I was at a basketball tournament. Their daughter, Natalie, was born that spring. They seemed happy, but I guess you never really know.

I started to date Emily in the summer of 2011. I didn't think that the fact that Johnny and Emily had dated was important, and both Johnny and Emily felt the same way. We went camping that summer, the four of us, and really had a good time. I thought that any possible problems in our friendship with each other were eliminated when Emily agreed to marry me after the camping trip. We were married the next summer.

I remember the last visit we had with Johnny. We had come to Wellington to help celebrate a friend's (Greg Carlisle) birthday. Johnny and his family were going to spend the night at my parents'

* The transcript of Paul Field's deposition was excerpted so that only his answers are reprinted here. Assume that this is a true and accurate rendering of those answers.

(Amy and Lonny) house. The guys were playing pool and then we went out for beers and food. Johnny seemed all right, but perhaps a little quiet. He was usually a pretty outgoing guy, but he just wasn't joking around too much that night. I talked with him about planning a hunting trip for October 28, but he seemed pretty quiet and told me that he wanted me to have his favorite shotgun for our hunting trip. I didn't understand then why he was acting that way and why he wanted to give me the shotgun, but I guess I know why now. I had a little too much beer, and Johnny carried me home. I thought he was going to stay overnight, but he was gone the next morning. My wife asked me if I thought everything was okay with Johnny, and I said that Johnny was acting kind of moody but that I would call him later to check up on him.

I tried to call Johnny all afternoon, but got no answer. At seven that night, Emily called Debi to see if Johnny was with her, but he wasn't. I kept on calling until about ten o'clock. At about 11:30, the phone rang and Emily answered it. She came into the living room and told me that Johnny was dead. I was blown away. She also told me what Johnny had told her the night before about Debi and that guy from work. Johnny was a careful driver. He wouldn't have driven onto a crossing if he knew the train was coming unless he wanted to kill himself. There's no doubt in my mind that if Johnny knew he was going to lose Debi and Natalie, he would choose not to live. I just wish he would have talked to me about the situation. Maybe I could have talked him out of it. Maybe I could have talked to Debi. Maybe I could have done something.

I don't want to have anything to do with Debi Fitzgerald, and I don't want my wife to either. If she agrees to testify that's her business, but I will not. I just hope that if Debi gets any money from this lawsuit some of it goes to Natalie, and not Debi and her mother. That's all I have to say.

It is hereby stipulated and agreed by and between the counsel for the respective parties that the reading and signing of the deposition by the witness are expressly waived by counsel and the witness and all objections are preserved until the time of trial.

I, Harold Bench, Notary Public and Court Reporter for the State of Nita, do certify that this deposition was taken telephonically, that Paul Field was sworn by me to tell the truth, and that his deposition was reduced to writing by me.

Harold Bench

Dated: April 28, 2014

Deposition of Amy Field*

April 14, 2014

My name is Amy Field. My birth date is May 26, 1964. I live at 905 Holiday in Wellington, Nita, with my husband, Lonny.

Yes, I did know Johnny Fitzgerald. Johnny was a friend of my son, Paul Field—who will be twenty-six on September 11—throughout high school and, in fact, was my son's best man at Paul's wedding, which was on July 4, 2012. During the wedding, I had an opportunity to talk with Johnny, and he told me how happy he was, having found the girl of his dreams, and how now with a daughter, he had lots to live for and really had it made.

On Friday, October 18, 2013, my son and his wife, Emily, and their four-month-old baby girl, Cameron, came to visit us from their home in Marion. They also came to help celebrate the birthday of Greg Carlisle, a high school friend of Paul and Johnny.

On Saturday, Johnny and his wife, Debi, and five-year-old daughter, Natalie, came to our house to see my son and his family. They were going to spend the night with us in the guestroom downstairs. Everyone seemed to be in good spirits. At about 6:00 p.m. Johnny, Paul, and Greg went to our basement to play pool, while Emily, Debi, and the children stayed upstairs watching television with me and my husband. At about 8:00 p.m., the boys decided to go out for some food and beers at Rocco's, a bar about five minutes away. At about 8:45 p.m., Emily and Debi went out to get some diapers for Emily's baby. I know it was right before nine o'clock because the store closes at nine. The store is about a mile away. They came back in about fifteen minutes, just after nine. Then Emily and Debi fed their daughters and decided to go up to Rocco's to meet the boys. They left about 9:30.

Emily called at about 10:45 p.m. to ask about the baby, just as the baby woke up. I told her the baby was up, and she and Debi came home, getting in about eleven o'clock. I went to sleep at 11:30, before the boys had come home. I didn't hear them come in.

* The transcript of Amy Field's deposition was excerpted so that only her answers are reprinted here. Assume that this is a true and accurate rendering of those answers.

When I woke up the next morning, Johnny and his family were gone and their bed was not slept in. Emily woke up and joined me in the kitchen. At about 10 a.m., Emily's cell phone rang. Emily said it was Debi. They talked for about five minutes, but I don't know what it was about.

Paul tried to call Johnny a few times during the afternoon. He said he wanted to check with Johnny about some good places for hunting that Johnny was going to look for. They were to go hunting the next week. He also said he wanted to check up on Johnny, but I wasn't sure what he meant by that.

At 11:30 that evening, the phone rang and woke me up. It was Debi's mother, Ethel Kay, asking to talk to Emily or Paul. I said that they were asleep, and she said to tell Paul and Emily that Johnny had died in a car accident. I was totally shocked. At this point, Emily came into the room and talked with Debi's mother.

A week or so after the funeral, I read a letter to the editor in the newspaper from Debi's mother, Ethel Kay. It said that the railroad was negligent in not making sure that the crossing was upgraded with flashing signals and bells, that someone had died, and that with the increased use of the road more people would die. I clipped out the letter and sent it to my son and daughter-in-law.

A few weeks ago, Emily called and told me she had given a deposition to the lawyers and was concerned about what was going on. I called Debi's mother and told her that Emily didn't want to hurt Debi or Natalie, and she said if Emily didn't want to hurt them she should stay out of it.

My son is still sad about losing Johnny and has said that he lost the best friend he ever had, just like losing a brother.

I have read this deposition, and the answers are correct to the best of my knowledge and belief.

Amy Field

Amy Field

Harold Bench

Harold Bench
Notary Public

April 14, 2014

Deposition of Nick Baron*

June 22, 2014

My name is Nick Baron. I live at 9225 Indian Creek Parkway, Nita City. I am sixty-six years old and retired. For the period September 2012 until January 2014, I was supervisor of welders at the Uprite Scaffolding plant in Wellington. As supervisor, it was my job to organize work schedules and make sure that my workers were doing their job.

I was Johnny Fitzgerald's supervisor at the plant. Before the plant opened, I knew Johnny from the old plant but did not come into regular contact with him. After we were both transferred to the new plant, we talked about scheduling. Johnny had requested the seven-to-three shift so that he could spend time with his daughter after he came home from work. Because he was a good worker, I agreed to his request.

Beginning in August 2013, Johnny's work habits became a little strange. Although he never came to work late before, he was late for work four times between September 15 and the date he died (October 20, 2013). The last time he was late, I thought I smelled alcohol on his breath, but Johnny said it was mouthwash. He explained that the reason he had been late recently was because his daughter had been ill and he needed to help take care of her in the mornings.

During the last month, he seemed a little distant and was not as outgoing as before, but I didn't think anything of it at the time. Everyone gets like that sometimes. We did talk about pheasant season, and I told him about some nice fields just south of the plant.

I used to live near the plant in Wellington. Before it was built, the only people who drove out in that area were people who lived out there and hunters. During construction, the crews started going out there more and once the plant opened, the roads got well traveled. Uprite employed 750 people at the plant for the day shift and 250 for the night shift. Sometimes I traveled on County Road across the tracks, but I never was there when the train crossed.

---

* The transcript of Nick Baron's deposition was excerpted so that only his answers are reprinted here. Assume that this is a true and accurate rendering of those answers.

I was sorry to hear about Johnny's death. He was a nice person.

I have read this deposition, and the answers are correct to the best of my knowledge and belief.

Nick Baron

Harold Bench
Notary Public

June 22, 2014

DX 30

Joshua Alan
Consulting Engineer

4747 Redmond Road/Nita City, Nita
49099/(555) 265-6500
JAlanConsult@NitaNet.nita

May 21, 2014

John Colton, Esq.
Colton & McLeod
Regency Plaza Suite 1300
Nita City, Nita 49099

Re: Fitzgerald v. Nita & Western Railroad

Dear John:

In connection with your request to examine the above-mentioned matter, I have had the opportunity to study the police report and the report compiled by the Nita & Western investigator, including the photos. I am especially impressed with the photo and description of the marks at the scene described by the trooper. In addition, I have today examined the scene of the collision.

Based upon the reports, photographs, and my examination, I have determined that the coefficient of friction for the surface of the road and the tires on the car was between.46 and.52. Using this coefficient of friction, and based upon an estimated speed of the car at the maximum speed limit of 50 mph, Mr. Fitzgerald's car should have left between 155 and 180 feet of skid marks had he locked his brakes. Assuming that it took between one-half and one second to react to the train (a reasonable reaction time), Mr. Fitzgerald's car would have traveled 37–74 feet before the brakes locked the wheels. These figures show that Mr. Fitzgerald had enough time to see the train, react, and apply his brakes in sufficient time to prevent the collision. Accordingly, in my opinion the railroad's maintenance of the foliage along the roadway for 250 feet was reasonable.

Based upon my experience in the field, the tests I have conducted on other cars and roads, as well as the information referred to above, it is my opinion that the marks on the road that were present at the time of the collision were a result of the car being dragged by the train upon impact. The marks were not skid marks. Indeed, there is no evidence that Mr. Fitzgerald ever applied his brakes. If there was an attempt to stop the car with the associated locking of brakes, then skid marks would have been in evidence.

Based upon the four hours I spent in this investigation, my charge for this report is $800. Thank you for the opportunity to consult on this matter.

Sincerely,

Joshua Alan
Consulting Engineer

DX 30

Skid Mark Charts

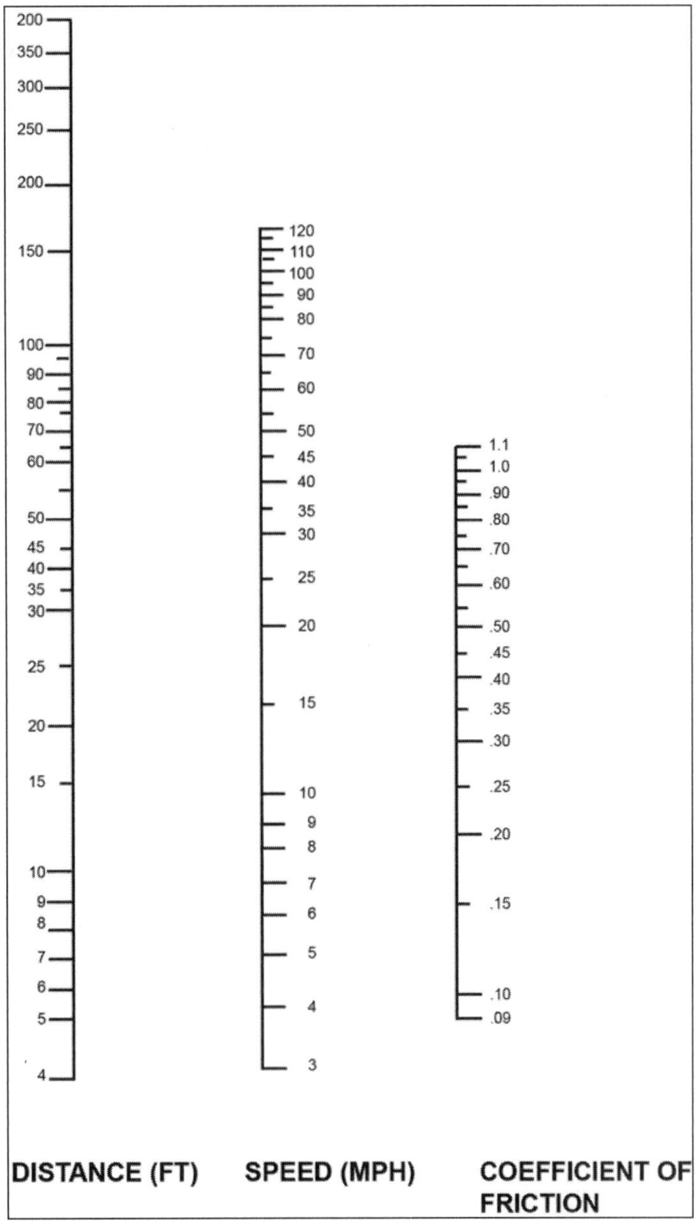

How to estimate speed from skid marks: Draw a straight line from the coefficient of friction to the average accident skid mark length.

DX 30

Skid Mark Charts

How to Determine the Coefficient of Friction

Example Problem: You have made a test skid in a vehicle traveling 30mph. The skid mark measurements are as follows:

Left Front = 60 feet   Left Rear = 57 feet
Right Front = 62 feet   Right Rear = 59 feet

Step 1 Add the lengths together
60 + 62 + 57 + 59 = 238

Step 2 Divide by 4 to find the average skidding distance
238 divided by 4 = 59.5

Step 3 Square the speed
30 x 30 = 900

Step 4 Divide 900 by 59.5 (distance or d)
900 divided by 59.5 = 15.13

Step 5 Multiply this by 0.033 (a constant)
15.13 x 0.033 = .4992 or .50

For Bias-Ply Tires Only

Coefficient of friction: Application for passenger cars and light-duty trucks with normal tire wear on relatively flat roads.

Road Condition	Coefficient
New asphalt, dry	85
New asphalt, wet	80
New concrete, dry	78
New concrete, wet	74
Old concrete, dry	63
Old concrete, wet	56
Old asphalt, dry	55
Old asphalt, wet	53
Good gravel, dry	52
Loose gravel, wet or dry	46
Tarred dirt, dry	40
Dirt, dry	36
Mud	28
Tarred dirt, wet	22
Packed snow (no chains)	20
Smooth ice (no chains)	9

If the vehicle has stopped on a hill or has excessively worn tires, or if the pavement conditions changed over the course of bringing the vehicle to a stop, this chart may not be used.

DX 31

Joshua Alan

Office Address:
4747 Redmond Road
Nita City, Nita
JAlanConsult@NitaNet.nita

Educational Background

- BS, Mechanical Engineering: University of Nita, 1990
- MS, Mechanical Engineering: University of Nita, 1991
- PhD, Mechanical Engineering: Massachusetts Institute of Technology, 1994

Employment

- Professor of Mechanical Engineering: University of Nita, since 2000
- State of Nita: Highway and Transportation Commission, 1994 to 2000

Consulting Fields

- Failure Analysis
- Highway Construction
- Products Liability
- Accident Reconstruction

Memberships

- American Society of Engineers
- National Society of Professional Engineers
- Nita State Engineering Society

Deposition of Steve Smolen[*]

March 19, 2014

My name is Steve Smolen. I was born in Nita City on June 25, 1975. I live at 449 Clearmeadow in Nita City. I am an engineer with the Nita & Western Railroad and have been with them for ten years. I worked for the Louisville & Nashville Railroad for ten years before that.

I am familiar with the crossing where the accident occurred, having been on that run for seven years. I go over that crossing five to six times each week. The crossing was protected by one cross-buck, on the eastern side. At the time of the collision, I thought it was a "farmer's crossing," meaning a private road going to a farmhouse. No one at Nita & Western ever told me that it was a county road crossing.

On October 20, 2013, I was the engineer on Train XT471 running from Lisle to Nita City. The train had four engines and eighty-five cars. The weather was clear and dry, although it was beginning to get dusky as it was getting closer to sundown. We got to the crossing about 5:45 p.m.

Q: Where were you as the train approached the crossing?

A: I was in the lead engine on the right side.

Q: Who was with you?

A: The conductor, Rich April. He was on the left side of the lead engine.

Q: Anyone else?

A: No. Matt Green, the brakeman, was in the second engine.

Q: Tell me everything that happened as you approached the crossing.

A: About a quarter-mile south of the crossing, we passed a whistle board, which signifies the beginning of a whistle sequence, so I began to blow the whistle.

---

* The transcript of Steve Smolen's deposition was excerpted so that, in some sections, only his answers are reprinted here. Assume that this is a true and accurate rendering of those answers.

Two longs, a short, and a long, repeated. There was nothing unusual during the crossing. After we passed the crossing about five car lengths, I started losing air on the engine.

Q: Before we get to that, I just want to make sure there was nothing else that happened before you got to the crossing other than blowing the whistle.

A: No, that's all I can remember.

Losing air was an indication that there was a break in the air line, and the brakes started setting up. I got the train to a complete stop and got out of the engine to look for the problem. The wheels on the boxcar were sideways on the track, and I saw what was left of a car on the tracks south of the engine portion of the train. The rest of the train was beyond the auto to the south. It had separated the boxes from the engines after the first box.

At the time of the collision, the whistle was blowing and the headlight was on.

Q: What was the lighting like as you approached the crossing where the accident occurred?

A: It was beginning to get dark, but it was still pretty light out. We had the headlights on, if that's what you're asking.

Q: Thank you. And what was your speed at that time?

A: We were traveling about forty-five to fifty miles per hour.

At that speed, it took me at least three-quarters of a mile to stop the train. There was no speed recorder and tape in the lead engine. I didn't know there was one in the second engine, but I now know that there was.

After the collision, Mark Edwards, the Nita & Western investigator, came to the site to collect our written reports and handle the matters with the trooper. We reattached the train at about 7:00 p.m. and continued on our route.

I was on the same track a few days later and noticed that the railroad had placed another crossbuck on the west side of the crossing.

During the period before the collision, I did not notice any appreciable increase in the number of cars crossing there. We usually came by at 5:15 to 6:00 in the evening and rarely saw any traffic there, especially on a Sunday.

Yes, I have been disciplined twice for excessive speed and failure to sound the whistle, but those charges were bogus. I have never been involved in a train accident before. As a result of the disciplinary action, I was especially sure that I would never speed or fail to sound the whistle.

I have read this deposition, and the answers are correct to the best of my knowledge and belief.

Steve Smolen

Steve Smolen

Harold Bench

Harold Bench
Notary Public

March 19, 2014

DX 32

Robert S. O'Sullivan, PhD
Consulting Forensic Economist

5620 S.W. 88th Avenue   Office: 515-855-9099
Nita City, Nita 49099   Fax: 515-855-9098
Robert@ROconsulting.nita

Sept. 29, 2014

Richard McLeod, Esquire
Jacob Clyde, Paralegal
Colton & McLeod
Regency Plaza, Suite 1300
Nita City, Nita 49099

Re: Economic Damages, Johnny Fitzgerald

Mr. McLeod:

At your request I have examined the economic facts presented in the Fitzgerald matter and Dr. Landsea's economic analysis of damages predicated upon those facts. My findings regarding Dr. Landsea's analysis are reported in detail below. Your request also was that I prepare an economic damage assessment using the conventional and generally acceptable methodology. I have prepared that and can report that the damage totals are more than 70% below those determined by Dr. Landsea.

My analysis of the appropriate damage valuations

By the conventional and generally accepted methodology the damage totals in present value terms were found to be:

	Past Loss	Future Loss	Total Loss
Lost Financial Support	$26,328	$657,598	$683,926
Lost Net Estate Accumulations	na	$15,857	$15,857
Lost Household Services	$9,078	$321,247	$330,324
TOTAL ALL LOSSES	$35,406	$994,702	$1,030,107

You will note that these values are about 70% smaller than Dr. Landsea's. Differences in assumptions about growth rates and discount rates are a part of the reason, but only a minor factor. My analysis used personal consumption rates (for the decedent) larger than those used by Dr. Landsea, hence less funds were available for financial support of the family. Consumption rates on both damage analysis reports were within the range used by most economists; mine were clearly more in the center of that range. My analysis projected savings not to be feasible until much later in Mr. Fitzgerald's working career. Thirty-something workers simply have no room in their budgets for saving. Conventional analysis expects material amounts of savings to begin to accumulate when workers reach age 50 or more.

Finally, the conventional analysis simply does not recognize those claimed lost services identified as "passive" by Dr. Landsea. Using the amount of services (14 hours a week) reported by the dependent family the damage calculations for lost services is reduced to just $330,324. This value is somewhat lower than the generally accepted source of service hours (American Time Use Survey) would have rendered. Dr. Landsea's valuation of lost services, in contrast, was in excess of $2,600,000.

My analysis of Dr. Landsea's evaluation of plaintiff Fitzgerald's damage claims

That analysis focused on three potential elements of economic loss typically examined in death cases. They included the estate's loss of estate accumulations and the dependent family's loss of the financial support and services normally provided by the decedent.

Dr. Landsea's overall approach to economic damage determination, excepting his analysis of household services lost, is consistent with methodology generally accepted and used by forensic economists. A review and replication of Dr. Landsea's damage calculations showed that his mathematics were correctly performed.

Damage calculations in the three areas of loss addressed by Dr. Landsea are explained below. Economic facts that might be challenged and questionable assumptions and calculations are identified.

Loss of financial support to dependent family

Financial support normally supplied by Mr. Fitzgerald to his family came solely from his gainful employment. His work as welder and his experience on the job resulted in wages that were projected by Dr. Landsea at $42,900 per year. Of that income, some would be taken as tax, some consumed by Mr. Fitzgerald himself, and some spent on necessary job expenses. Any family savings would have come from that income as well. The balance would be funds available for financial support of the dependent family.

Lost financial support was calculated to the end of a normal worklife at age 65. Dr. Landsea relies upon United States Department of Labor projections that show the average male worker remaining in the workforce to that age. Those projections do not, however, support Dr. Landsea's implicit assumption of Mr. Fitzgerald's continuous full-time, year-round employment as welder to age 65. In fact, it may be discovered from Mr. Fitzgerald's work history to date of death that his employment pattern showed considerable periods of time with no or with lessor paid employment. A finding of say 10% annual gaps could very well be used for an argument to reduce projected losses in the same proportions. At 10%, that reduction would equal $112,500 in present value terms. Similar reductions would be had in the calculation of net lost estate accumulations, as they too arise from wages earned in an average year of employment.

In addition to the potential dollar reduction in calculated loss amounts, the discovery of a spotty employment history may be used to challenge Dr. Landsea's motive for his seemingly uncritical assumption of full-time, year-round employment in Mr. Fitzgerald's future. (Note that the forensic economist is not an investigator and is not normally charged with the duty of independently discovering relevant economic facts about the subject person.)

The assumption of a normal worklife might also be challenged in several productive ways. Any challenge acting to reduce the worklife would, of course, benefit the defendants by reducing the dollar amount of lost future support and its present value. In this case, Mr. Fitzgerald found employment as a welder—an occupation requiring significant amounts of physical capacity and practice skills. At age 25 Mr. Fitzgerald appeared to possess both. The challenge to Dr. Landsea is to demonstrate that welders in general, and Mr. Fitzgerald in particular, would normally possess both in sufficient measure to be employed for another 40 years. The fact is that males alive at age 25 will not all survive to age 65, much less all be physically and mentally fit to function as a welder. Dr. Landsea will be unlikely to be prepared with survival data by year. It may be true that some average workers leave their jobs before age 65 but others do stay on the job well past age 65. On balance then, his assumption of employment to age 65 can be defended as economically reasonable under the "certainty equivalent" method.

One other version of the challenge could be mounted if something about the welder occupation militates against long-term careers. Other indirect influences collectively called life contingencies might be argued. Will Mr. Fitzgerald continue to qualify for a driver's license to transport himself to work? Will his health continuously remain sufficiently good to allow full-time employment? Will the job classification of welder continue to be in demand in the labor market? Will his labor market continue to offer employment opportunities for welders?

Institutional factors such as pension plans allowing for "early" retirement might suggest able-bodied persons leaving the workforce at ages well below 65. Retirement planning by the worker may at least reveal the potential for early retirement. If Mr. Fitzgerald had planned to retire at age 58, for example, then his dependents can hardly argue that his death has taken away financial support expected from him at ages 59-65.

<u>Loss of expected net estate accumulations (savings)</u>

All the above arguments regarding reducing the estimates of lost financial support would apply as well here. Potential savings as well as family financial support arise from the worker's income earnings. Future savings that do not occur due to the worker's death at age 25 are the genesis of lost estate accumulations assumed to be realized at the end of a normal life expectancy. Given whatever income earnings are projected, some productive questioning of Dr. Landsea's savings assumptions and calculations is still possible. These are outlined below.

First, the percentage of income likely to be saved is known to be highly correlated to income levels and family size. At lower income levels, family living expenses need take precedence over and eventually overwhelm the desire to save. As pointed out above, a reasonable argument may develop to reduce the income levels projected by Dr. Landsea for Mr. Fitzgerald. A drop of 10 to 20% in the projected $42,900 income levels may well be enough to eliminate the prospects for any savings. Prospects for a larger family size would also. However a larger family size by itself would only tend to shift dollars of loss from the lost net accumulations category to the lost family financial support category. A reduction only in income levels could eliminate savings potential as well, but more importantly for defendants would reduce the total dollars available for financial support.

Second, it may well be discovered that at the date of his death Mr. Fitzgerald was saving little or nothing from his wages. Many employers do not offer either pension plans or voluntary savings schemes such of 401(k) plans. Discovery of Mr. Fitzgerald's employment terms may provide information to that effect to allow challenge to Dr. Landsea's assumption that 5% would have been saved from wages from the date of his death onward. Also it may be discovered that Mr. Fitzgerald had no ongoing savings program of his own. Thus, allowing the same challenge and perhaps leading to questions to Dr. Landsea regarding why he did not bother to make himself knowledgeable about this subject.

Loss of Household Services

The death of a service provider can lead to significant losses to the service beneficiaries—in this case, Mr. Fitzgerald's wife and daughter. The typical economic analysis of such damages is based on a projection of services normally rendered and the amount of time devoted to each. Normally rendered services are either specifically identified by the dependent family and/or discovered from studies such as the American Time Use Survey (ATUS - United States Department of Labor). This and other similar studies report results of surveys identifying and quantifying services rendered by average adult members of households.

In this case, Dr. Landsea has used information provided by the family about ACTIVE services normally provided by Mr. Fitzgerald. Active services typically are household chores, and in this case childcare; they are essentially all that ATUS reports on. Mr. Fitzgerald's time and effort apparently reported by the family is somewhat less than that reported in ATUS. Challenging damage calculations based on those hours of effort reported by the family therefore would not be productive. However, it could be argued that as family size decreases in the future and as Mr. Fitzgerald ages, the required number and amount of service effort he might produce can be expected to diminish. Note that even a 10% decline in expected future active services will reduce the present value calculation of lost active services by $43,550.

Another category of services identified by Dr. Landsea as PASSIVE services is introduced in the damage calculations. Passive services are rarely, if ever, seen in economic damage evaluations—perhaps because the authoritative sources such as ATUS do not feature these as areas of services normally rendered to the household. Dr. Landsea's analysis assumes that they are necessary services rendered in a passive manner by Mr. Fitzgerald. These services are identified as passive because the service provider is not often, or sometimes ever, providing an active service during the passive service hours. A typical passive service is rendered while the service provider is sleeping or otherwise tending to personal needs. Thus, a sleeping parent is there for the protection of sleeping infant children and to render the occasional need for active services such as diaper changing during the night. Because passive services are being rendered at all times when the service provider and family members are together in the household, many hours a day are involved. The replacement cost of labor customarily used to value lost services, even at minimum wages, therefore accumulates to very large present value amounts.

Arguments to reduce these damage estimates fall into two main categories: one simply asserts that conventional damage analysis does not recognize passive damages and that passive damage therefore should not be gratuitously introduced here; the other argument suggests that because he is part of a parental team, the loss of Mr. Fitzgerald's passive effort is not material to the child as a passive service beneficiary.

Law in most states does not explicitly call for compensation for lost passive services. Typically, the laws merely say that "lost services" are compensable. In one state, Florida, statutes do provide compensation for loss of "protection" by surviving spouses. In that circumstance, defendants are reduced to arguing about the nature and cost of replacement protection: Guard dog? Alarm service? Security officer? Dr. Landsea's valuation approach assumes the most costly: the employment of a human security agent.

Other Critical Elements of Economic Methodology

Every forensic economist incorporates values for inflation, cost and wage growth, and discount interest rates into the valuation methodology. When inputted into the damage calculations, each of these economic variables will have very material effects on the bottom-line damage findings. This is particularly true in cases like Fitzgerald, where losses are projected many years into the future. Some of the values attached to the variables are presented simply as economic fact; some are clearly identified as the economist's opinion. Even the variables identified as economic facts are discovered and used by the economist in a judgmental manner. Other forensic economists use similar expressions of their professional judgment in selecting values for these critical elements of damage calculations. In most states, no state statute or rule requires particular values to be used for any of these critical values.

Dr. Landsea uses values for these economic variables that fall within what typically is identified as the "normal" range of values presented by most forensic economists. As it happens, his selected values tend to fit close to midpoint in those ranges. It would be difficult, therefore, to be overly critical of his choice of values. A more productive approach would focus on the mathematics associated with values found higher or lower in the ranges. Demonstrating that input variables other than Dr. Landsea's can significantly reduce the present value of losses could lead to a discussion about the fact that other forensic economists do routinely use those values, and that other reasonable choices of economic inputs will act to produce lower damage calculations. This may leave the finder-in-fact with alternative lower loss values to consider.

For example, Dr. Landsea used a 3.3% discount rate to arrive at the present values of loss totaling $3,500,000. He would agree that a 1% higher (4.3%) discount rate would result mathematically with a dramatically lower present value ($2,200,000). I currently use a 3.6% discount rate. Likewise, Dr. Landsea made a 2% forecast of future inflation. A 1% lower forecast for future inflation would in itself reduce the present value of losses to $1,900,000. Both a 1% higher discount rate and a 1% lower inflation rate would reduce the calculated present value of loss to just $1,450,000.

Periodic surveys of professional forecasters do show that a significant percentage of them would agree with the use of these 1% different economic input values. Dr. Landsea knows that and would likely agree that other forensic economists could well look at the economic circumstances in Fitzgerald and arrive at the lower present values discussed above.

The discussion above covers areas in which I believe Dr. Landsea's opinions of economic damage are most likely to be reduced by proper challenging of economic facts and presentation of alternative damage calculations. Other more technical criticisms of his work are possible, but are not likely to produce information the finder-of-fact would have any interest in or real ability to understand outside the unwanted "gradate course in economics" approach.

If your case requires it, I can prepare you for deposition questioning of Dr. Landsea and/or for cross-examination should the case come to court. Please review this letter and call me with further questions or concerns.

Please treat this letter as my request for payment of my fee for my service to date; 10 hours at $475 per hour ($4,750). Attached please find my professional CV.

Respectfully yours,

Robert S. O'Sullivan, PhD
Consulting Forensic Economist

DX 33

Robert S. O'Sullivan, PhD
Consulting Forensic Economist

5620 S.W. 88th Avenue Office: 515-855-9099
Nita City, Nita 49099 Fax: 515-855-9098
Robert@ROconsulting.nita

EDUCATION

- BS, 1971, University of Nita
- MBA, 1974, University of Nita
- PhD, 1978, University of Nita

EXPERIENCE

- Instructor, University of Nita, 1974–1978
- Assistant Professor, University of Illinois, 1978–1983
- Associate Professor, University of Illinois, 1983–1988
- Professor, University of Nita, 1988–present

CONSULTING

- Exxon, 1983–1985
- Dow Chemical, 1987–90
- Expert Witness, Economics and Damages, 1990–present

SELECTED PUBLICATIONS AND PRESENTATIONS

- *Growth Trends in Wages and Fringe Benefit Packages in Industrial Enterprises*, Annual Meeting of the CPDE, Las Vegas NV, March 2013
- *The Gender Gap and Age-Earnings of Attorneys, Physicians and Engineers*, 2010 Annual Meeting of the American Academy of Economic and Financial Experts, Las Vegas NV, March 2010
- Forensic Economics, A Contemporary Approach, LexisNexis (6th Edition 2013)

Applicable Nita Statutes

Motor Vehicles: Chapter 89

Section 71. Obedience to signal indicating approach of train. (a) Whenever any person driving a vehicle approaches a railroad crossing under any of the circumstances stated in this section, the driver of such vehicle shall stop within fifty (50) feet but not less than fifteen (15) feet from the nearest rail of such railroad, and shall not proceed until he or she can do so safely. The foregoing requirements shall apply when:

1. A clearly visible electric or mechanical signal device gives warning of the immediate approach of a railroad train;
2. A crossing gate is lowered or when a human flagman gives or continues to give a signal of the approach or passage of a railroad train;
3. A railroad train approaching within approximately one thousand two hundred (1,200) feet of the highway crossing emits a signal audible from such distance and such railroad train, by reason of its speed or nearness to such crossing, is an immediate hazard; or
4. An approaching railroad train is plainly visible and is in hazardous proximity to such crossing.

Public Utilities: Chapter 66

Section 120. Failure of locomotive to sound whistle at crossing. An air whistle shall be attached to each locomotive engine, and shall be sounded four (4) times (two long, one short, one long) beginning at least 1,200 feet from where the railroad shall cross any public road and shall be repeated until the crossing is occupied by the engine, under penalty of a fine of $100 for every neglect of the provisions of this section.

Section 212. Duty to maintain foliage at crossings. All railroads shall maintain the foliage along roads which intersect railroad tracks by mowing and clearing sufficiently to permit a motorist to observe an oncoming train from a distance appropriate to the allowable speed of the roadway.

Wrongful Death: Chapter 70

Section 1. Liability. When the death of a person is caused by the wrongful act, negligence, default, or breach of contract or warranty of any person, including those occurring on navigable waters, and the event would have entitled the person injured to maintain an action and recover damages if death had not ensued, the person or watercraft that would have been liable in damages if death had not ensued shall be liable for damages as specified in this act notwithstanding the death of the person injured, although death was caused under circumstances constituting a felony.

Section 2. Damages. All potential beneficiaries of a recovery for wrongful death, including the decedent's estate, shall be identified in the complaint, and their relationships to the decedent shall be alleged. Damages may be awarded as follows:

1. Each survivor may recover the value of lost support and services from the date of the decedent's injury to her or his death, with interest, and future loss of support and services from the date of death and reduced to present value. In evaluating loss of support and services, the survivor's

relationship to the decedent, the amount of the decedent's probable net income available for distribution to the particular survivor, and the replacement value of the decedent's services to the survivor may be considered. In computing the duration of future losses, the joint life expectancies of the survivor and the decedent and the period of minority, in the case of healthy minor children, may be considered.

2. The surviving spouse may also recover for loss of the decedent's companionship and protection and for mental pain and suffering from the date of injury.
3. Minor children of the decedent, and all children of the decedent if there is no surviving spouse, may also recover for lost parental companionship, instruction, and guidance, and for mental pain and suffering from the date of injury. For the purposes of this subsection, if both spouses die within thirty days of one another as a result of the same wrongful act or series of acts arising out of the same incident, each spouse is considered to have been predeceased by the other.
4. Each parent of a deceased minor child may also recover for mental pain and suffering from the date of injury. Each parent of an adult child may also recover for mental pain and suffering if there are no other survivors.
5. Medical or funeral expenses due to the decedent's injury or death may be recovered by a survivor who has paid them.
6. The decedent's personal representative may recover for the decedent's estate the loss of earnings of the deceased from the date of injury to the date of death, less lost support of survivors excluding contributions in kind, with interest. Loss of the prospective net accumulations of an estate, which might reasonably have been expected but for the wrongful death, reduced to present money value, may also be recovered if the decedent's survivors include a surviving spouse or lineal descendants.

Comparative Negligence: Chapter 140

Section 3. Contributory Negligence No Bar to Recovery of Damages. In all actions hereafter brought for personal injuries, or where such injuries have resulted in death, or for injury to property, the fact that the person injured, or the owner of the property, or the person having control over the property may have been guilty of contributory negligence shall not bar a recovery, but damages shall be diminished by the jury in proportion to the amount of negligence attributable to the person injured, or the owner of the property, or the person having control over the property.

Proposed Jury Instructions

Preliminary Instruction 1: Introduction

You have been selected as jurors and have taken an oath to well and truly try this cause. This trial will last one day. During the progress of the trial, there will be periods of time when the Court recesses. During those periods of time, you must not talk about this case amongst yourselves or with anyone else.

During the trial, do not talk to any of the parties, their lawyers, or any of the witnesses. If any attempt is made by anyone to talk to you concerning the matters here under consideration, you should immediately report that fact to the Court.

You should keep an open mind. You should not form or express an opinion during the trial and should reach no conclusion in this case until you have heard all of the evidence, the arguments of counsel, and the final instructions as to the law that will be given to you by the Court.

Preliminary Instruction 2: Conduct of the Trial

First, the attorneys will have an opportunity to make opening statements. These statements are not evidence and should be considered only as a preview of what the attorneys expect the evidence will be.

Following the opening statements, witnesses will be called to testify. They will be placed under oath and questioned by the attorneys. Documents and other tangible exhibits may also be received as evidence. If an exhibit is given to you to examine, you should examine it carefully, individually, and without any comment.

It is counsel's right and duty to object when testimony or other evidence is being offered that he or she believes is not admissible. When the Court sustains an objection to a question, the jurors must disregard the question and the answer, if one has been given, and draw no inference from the question or answer or speculate as to what the witness would have said if permitted to answer. Jurors must also disregard evidence stricken from the record.

When the Court sustains an objection to any evidence, the jurors must disregard that evidence. When the Court overrules an objection to any evidence, the jurors must not give that evidence any more weight than if the objection had not been made.

When the evidence is completed, the attorneys will make final statements. These final statements are not evidence but are given to assist you in evaluating the evidence. The attorneys are also permitted to argue in an attempt to persuade you to a particular verdict. You may accept or reject those arguments as you see fit.

Finally, just before you retire to consider your verdict, I will give you further instructions on the law that applies to this case.

FINAL INSTRUCTIONS (GENERAL)

Members of the jury, the evidence in this case has been completed, and I will now instruct you as to the law.

The law applicable to this case is stated in these instructions, and it is your duty to follow all of them. You must not single out certain instructions and disregard others.

It is your duty to determine the facts, and to determine them only from the evidence in this case. You are to apply the law to the facts and in this way decide the case. You must not be governed or influenced by sympathy or prejudice for or against any party in this case. Your verdict must be based on evidence and not upon speculation, guess, or conjecture.

From time to time, the court has ruled on the admissibility of evidence. You must not concern yourselves with the reasons for these rulings. You should disregard questions and exhibits that were withdrawn or to which objections were sustained.

You should also disregard testimony and exhibits that the court has refused or stricken.

The evidence that you should consider consists only of the witnesses' testimonies and the exhibits the court has received.

Any evidence that was received for a limited purpose should not be considered by you for any other purpose.

You should consider all the evidence in the light of your own observations and experiences in life.

Neither by these instructions nor by any ruling or remark that I have made do I mean to indicate any opinion as to the facts or as to what your verdict should be.

Opening statements are made by the attorneys to acquaint you with the facts they expect to prove. Closing arguments are made by the attorneys to discuss the facts and circumstances in the case, and should be confined to the evidence and to reasonable inferences to be drawn therefrom. Neither opening statements nor closing arguments are evidence, and any statement or argument made by the attorneys that is not based on the evidence should be disregarded.

You are the sole judges of the credibility of the witnesses and of the weight to be given to the testimony of each witness. In determining what credit is to be given any witness, you may take into account his or her ability and opportunity to observe; his or her manner and appearance while testifying; any interest, bias, or prejudice he or she may have; the reasonableness of the testimony considered in the light of all the evidence; and any other factors that bear on the believability and weight of the witness's testimony.

You have heard evidence in this case from witnesses who testified as experts. The law allows experts to express an opinion on subjects involving their special knowledge, training and skill, experience, or research. While their opinions are allowed to be given, it is entirely within the province of the jury to determine what weight shall be given their testimony. Jurors are not bound by the testimony of experts; their testimony is to be weighed as that of any other witness.

The law recognizes two kinds of evidence: direct and circumstantial. Direct evidence proves a fact directly; that is, the evidence by itself, if true, establishes the fact. Circumstantial evidence is the proof of facts or circumstances that give rise to a reasonable inference of other facts; that is, circumstantial evidence proves a fact indirectly in that it follows from other facts or circumstances according to common experience and observations in life. An eyewitness is a common example of direct evidence, while human footprints are circumstantial evidence that a person was present.

The law makes no distinction between direct and circumstantial evidence as to the degree or amount of proof required, and each should be considered according to whatever weight or value it may have. All of the evidence should be considered and evaluated by you in arriving at your verdict.

Final Instructions (Specific)

1. The Court will now instruct you on the claims and defenses of each party and the law that will apply to the case. You must arrive at your verdict by applying the law as you now receive it to the facts of the case.

2. The parties to this case are Debra Fitzgerald, on her own behalf, as the mother of Natalie Fitzgerald and as the administrator of the Estate of Johnny Fitzgerald, as plaintiffs, and the Nita & Western Railroad Co., as defendant.

3. The defendant has admitted in the pleadings, and you must regard as conclusively proven, the following:

    a. On October 20, 2013, Johnny Fitzgerald was operating his car on County Road in Douglas County, Nita, traveling easterly and approaching Nita & Western rail crossing #74647C. At the intersection of County Road and the Nita & Western tracks, Johnny Fitzgerald's car and the Nita & Western train collided. Johnny Fitzgerald died as a result of injuries sustained in the collision. On November 15, 2013, Debra Fitzgerald was appointed the administratrix of the Estate of Johnny Fitzgerald. Johnny Fitzgerald was survived by Debra Fitzgerald, his wife, and by Natalie Fitzgerald, his daughter.

    b. The plaintiffs claim that Nita & Western was negligent in its operation of the train or by its failure to warn Johnny Fitzgerald of the oncoming train, and that its negligence caused Johnny Fitzgerald's injuries and death. The plaintiffs seek damages for the defendant's negligence on behalf of herself individually, her daughter, and the estate. The defendant denies that Nita & Western was negligent and claims that Johnny Fitzgerald was either negligent or that he intentionally drove his car into the train, causing his injuries and death.

4. In this case, the plaintiffs have the burden of proving by a preponderance of the evidence that Nita & Western was negligent by:

    a. operating the train at an unsafe speed; or

    b. failing to keep an adequate lookout; or

    c. failing to sound its whistle or shine its headlamp; or

    d. failing to adequately notify that a crossing was present and a train was coming; or

    e. failing to properly maintain foliage on the intersecting roadway approaching the crossing; and that any such negligence was a proximate cause of Johnny Fitzgerald's death.

5. The defendant has the burden of proving by a preponderance of the evidence that Johnny Fitzgerald was negligent in failing to maintain a proper lookout or that Johnny Fitzgerald intentionally took his own life, and that such failure or intentional acts were a proximate cause of his death.

6. Thus, each of the parties has a burden of proof to maintain, and you are to determine whether they have met their burdens. Your task is to determine whether Johnny Fitzgerald or the Nita & Western Railroad, or both of them, were negligent and the extent to which their respective negligence caused the death of Johnny Fitzgerald, or whether Johnny Fitzgerald committed suicide.

7. By "a preponderance of the evidence," I mean that you must be persuaded from a consideration of all of the evidence in the case that the issue is more probably true than not true.

8. The terms "negligence" or "negligent" as used in these instructions mean the failure to use that degree of care that an ordinarily prudent person would use under the same or similar circumstances.

9. The terms "contributory negligence" or "contributorily negligent" mean negligence on the part of Johnny Fitzgerald.

10. Violations of a statute of the State of Nita, if you find such violations, are negligence as a matter of law. Such negligence has the same effect as any other acts of negligence.

11. It is the duty of a railroad company to use such care and precaution as ordinary prudence dictates. It must exercise greater care and vigilance in areas of more frequent crossings than in areas of less frequent crossings. The degree of care that the law requires to be exercised must be commensurate with the probability of danger. The railway crew must maintain a proper lookout and maintain proper control of the train. Proper lookout and control are such lookout and control as will avoid collision with cars being operated without negligence. While maintaining a lookout, the crew may assume that a driver of a car will bring the car to a stop until such time as it becomes apparent that the driver is not going to stop.

12. A statute of the State of Nita requires that an air whistle of a train be sounded at least 1,200 feet from a railroad crossing and continue until the engine crosses the roadway, and shall consist of four sounds: two longs, one short, and then one long.

13. A statute of the State of Nita provides that it is the duty of a railroad company to maintain the foliage along roads that intersect railroad tracks by mowing and clearing sufficiently to permit a motorist traveling along the road to observe a train approaching the crossing from a distance appropriate to the allowable speed of the roadway.

14. It is the duty of the driver of a car to keep a proper lookout and have his car under proper control to avoid collisions or accidents, assuming other drivers are exercising ordinary care.

15. A statute of the State of Nita requires that a driver of a car approaching a railroad crossing shall stop at least fifteen feet before the crossing and not proceed until he can do so safely under the following circumstances:

    a. A railroad train approaching the crossing emits an audible sound within 1,200 feet of the crossing and the train by reason of its speed or nearness is an immediate hazard; or

    b. An approaching train is clearly visible and is in hazardous proximity to the crossing.

16. It is the duty of a driver approaching a railroad crossing to look and listen at a time and place where looking and listening would be effective. Failure of the railroad to give signals at a railroad crossing does not relieve one about to cross a crossing from the duty to use due care to look and listen for an approaching train.

17. In a death action, where there is no direct evidence as to an accident causing fatal injury, facts and circumstances may be proven by circumstantial evidence. Unless the defendant establishes to the contrary by a preponderance of the evidence, the law requires you to assume that the instincts of natural love of life and hesitancy to die prevailed in the mind of Johnny Fitzgerald just prior to his

death. If the preponderance of the evidence is that the death of Johnny Fitzgerald was attributable to his intentional act or omission, undertaken with an intent to commit suicide, then you are instructed to indicate this finding.

18. Proximate cause is that cause that, in the natural and continuous sequence, produces the injury, and without which the injury would not have occurred. To be a proximate cause of Johnny Fitzgerald's death, negligent conduct on the part of Johnny Fitzgerald or Nita & Western need not be the only cause nor the last cause. It is sufficient if the negligent con- duct acting concurrently with another cause produced the injury. Thus, there need not be only one proximate cause.

19. In the State of Nita, we have what is called a "pure comparative negligence" statute. The law provides that:

    In all actions hereafter brought for personal injuries, or where such injuries have resulted in death, . . . the fact that the person injured . . . may have been guilty of contributory negligence shall not bar a recovery, but damages shall be diminished by the jury in proportion to the amount of negligence attributable to the person injured.

20. What this means is that the contributory negligence of Johnny Fitzgerald, if any, would not bar the plaintiff's recovery. The law directs you to apportion the responsibility and, thus, the damages in accordance with the relative fault of the parties. Therefore, the damages allowed to be recovered by the plaintiffs should be diminished in proportion to the amount of negligence that was a legal cause of the deceased's death and that was attributable to the deceased, whether or not such negligence is greater than that of the defendant.

21. You are to determine the negligence, if any, of both Johnny Fitzgerald and Nita & Western Railroad, and then to apportion the responsibility of each. Please state your findings of negligence in the following form:

    We find the conduct of the defendant, Nita & Western Railroad, was

    ______% negligent.

    We find the conduct of the deceased, Johnny Fitzgerald, was

    ______% negligent.

    The percentages must total 100%.

22. In this case, you must also decide the issue of damages. You must determine the amount of damages that will reasonably and fairly compensate Debra Fitzgerald and Natalie Fitzgerald for the losses resulting from the death of Johnny Fitzgerald. In determining the loss, you should consider the following factors:

    a. The reasonable funeral expenses of the decedent;

    b. The present monetary value of the decedent to the persons entitled to receive damages recovered, including, but not limited to, compensation for the loss of the reasonably expected;

    c. net income of the decedent;

    d. services, protection, care, and assistance of the decedent, whether voluntary or obligatory, to the persons entitled to the damages recovered;

e. society, companionship, comfort, guidance, kindly offices, and advice of the decedent to the persons entitled to the damages recovered;

f. Nominal damages when the jury so finds.

23. In determining the amount of damages to the plaintiffs, you may consider how long the decedent was likely to have lived, that some persons work all their lives and that others do not, and that a person's earnings may remain the same, increase, or decrease in the future.

IN THE CIRCUIT COURT OF
DOUGLAS COUNTY, NITA
CIVIL DIVISION

DEBRA FITZGERALD, Administratrix of the Estate JOHNNY FITZGERALD, and DEBRA FITZGERALD, individually and on behalf of her minor child Natalie FITZGERALD Plaintiffs v. NITA & WESTERN RAILROAD CO. Defendant	))))))))))))))	VERDICT

The jury is to answer the following questions. The foreperson is to answer the questions for the jury and sign the verdict.

1. Was the death of Johnny Fitzgerald attributable to his intentional act or omission, undertaken with an intent to commit suicide?

   Yes ______ No ______

If your answer to question 1 is yes, you need not continue your deliberations and should return to Court.

2. Do you find that either Johnny Fitzgerald or the Nita & Western Railroad were negligent?

   Yes ______ No ______

If your answer to question 2 is no, you need not continue your deliberations and should return to Court.

3. Please state your findings of negligence in the following form:

   We find the conduct of the defendant, Nita & Western Railroad, was___________% negligent.

   We find the conduct of the deceased, Johnny Fitzgerald, was___________% negligent.

   The percentages must total 100%.

4. Please determine the total amount of damages to the plaintiffs, without regard to the amount of negligence attributable to either party.

____

The Court will multiply the percentage of negligence that you find to be apportioned to the defendant, Nita & Western Railroad (question 3), by the amount of total damages you have determined (question 4), and that amount shall be the verdict for the plaintiffs.

____

Foreperson

Special Impeachment Problems

Problems 1, 2, 3, and 4 are designed to be used in conjunction with the special impeachment slides that come with the PowerPoint slide show in order to learn how to integrate technology into the impeachment process. There are several options for display that accompany the transcript segment for each witness: (1) the written Q and A only; (2) the video only; (3) the video with transcript; (4) a photo taken of the deponent with transcript; (5) the Q and A revealing one at a time.

Problem 1: Debra Fitzgerald

Assume the following exchange occurred at trial during the direct examination of Debra Fitzgerald:

Q: When you talked to Emily Field on the morning of October 20, did she say anything to you about what Johnny and Emily had talked about the night before?

Defense Counsel: Objection, your Honor. This is hearsay.

Plaintiff Counsel: It goes to Johnny's state of mind.

Judge: Overruled.

A: Yes, she said that they had talked about Johnny's upcoming birthday. Johnny had said he was looking forward to the party. She told me that she had asked Johnny what he wanted as a present, and Johnny said he really wanted a new hunting jacket, as he and Paul were going to go hunting the following week. She asked me if I was going to get him a new jacket, and if I wasn't, she would get one for him as a present. I told her that I'd bought him something else.

a) For the defendant, cross-examine Mrs. Fitzgerald based upon this portion of her testimony.

b) For the plaintiffs, conduct any necessary redirect examination.

Problem 2: Debra Fitzgerald

Assume the following answer was given at trial during the direct examination of Debra Fitzgerald:

> "A little while after Johnny and Natalie came back from their walk, I headed off to my parents' house along with Natalie and a load of laundry I had in a laundry bag. We left about 12:30."

a) For the defendant, cross-examine Mrs. Fitzgerald based upon this portion of her testimony.

b) For the plaintiffs, conduct any necessary redirect examination.

Problem 3: Steve Smolen

Assume the following exchange occurred at trial during the direct examination of Mr. Smolen:

Q: As you approached the crossing, where were you?

A: I was in the lead engine on the right side. Rich April was in the lead engine on the left side.

Q: What happened next?

A: Right before the crossing, Rich said something like, "He's crazy." I could hardly hear him due to the engine. Then the engine started to lose air.

a) For the plaintiffs, cross-examine Mr. Smolen based upon this portion of his testimony.

b) For the defendant, conduct any necessary redirect examination.

Problem 4: Steve Smolen

Assume the following answer was given at trial during the direct examination of Steve Smolen:

> "At the time we approached the crossing, we had our headlight on, were blowing our whistle, and were traveling no more than thirty-five to forty miles per hour."

(a) For the plaintiffs, cross-examine Mr. Smolen based upon this portion of his testimony.

(b) For the defendant, conduct any necessary redirect examination.